An Inward STILLNESS

Wendy C. Top & Brent L. Top

BOOKCRAFT
Salt Lake City, Utah

Library of Congress Catalog Card Number: 95-75272

ISBN 0-88494-978-8

First Printing, 1995

Printed in the United States of America

Let us then labor for an inward stillness,
An inward stillness and an inward healing,
That perfect silence where the lips and heart
Are still, and we no longer entertain
Our own imperfect thought and vain opinions,
But God alone speaks in us, and we wait
In singleness of heart, that we may know
His will, and in the silence of our spirits,
That we may do His will, and do that only!

—Henry Wadsworth Longfellow

Contents

Contents

Preface

Some people have been surprised and even a little uncomfortable with our openness in speaking honestly about the personal struggles revealed in this book. (Wendy wanted to call it "True Confessions of a Molly Mormon.") However, they have seemed grateful to discover that they are not alone in the frustration and even resentment they sometimes feel about the unrealistic and unrelenting expectations they perceive as being placed upon them by the surrounding Mormon culture.

In recent years we, as a people, have become more aware of this problem and have begun to address it from the pulpit and in print. We have finally begun to think and speak differently, but many of the old tendencies are deeply ingrained and very subtle and have not yet been fully overcome. We have wondered if the problems were created by our own mistaken overemphasis on works and an almost condescending attitude about grace. In the beginning of his presidency, President Ezra Taft Benson chided the Saints for the darkness of mind resting on them because they had treated lightly the Book of Mormon (see "The Book of Mormon—Keystone of Our Religion," *Ensign*, November 1986, p. 7; see also D&C 84:54–57). Perhaps our misunderstanding of grace as plainly set forth in that sacred book was a large part of that darkness. As we made greater use of the book, the passages and doctrines on grace began to emerge; it was almost as if we couldn't see them before. Because of this emergence, we are beginning to develop to a higher level of understanding, obedience, and behavior—from living by the letter or works only to living by the Spirit or grace and faith.

The Church will achieve this higher order only as individual members experience this change in their own lives. To that end we have written this book and shared our personal struggles. We don't have all the answers, but we hope that our experiences may lead others to their own desired transformation and the inward stillness and fulfillment that such real gospel living can bring.

Wendy C. Top
Brent L. Top

Chapter One

"The Kingdom of God Is Within You"

Lessons Learned from Trying Too Hard

*N*ow that Wendy's battle with clinical depression is under control, she can say that it was a great blessing to her. In the midst of the fray we were desperately questioning God's wisdom, but as the clouds of pain disperse and clear thinking returns we see it as a mid-course correction from a loving Pilot who did not want her to miss her destination.

That destination, of course, is exaltation. Yet Wendy, like many others, felt that the only way she could get there was by being perfect—now. She laughed along with others who poked fun at "Patty Perfect" and the impossibility of being all things to all people. Yet subtly, over a period of thirty-four years, she had programmed her mind one item at a time with lists of "shoulds" and "oughts" that she thought were essential to being faithful. For instance, she would see Sister Jones with all her lovely children and think, "I should have more children, like Sister Jones." Hearing that Sister Smith was always the first one to give a baby shower or take in a meal when someone was sick, she would think, "I should render compassionate service like Sister Smith." She was amazed at Sister Martin's dedication to genealogical research, who would often remind us that it is the greatest work the Lord has laid upon us; and Wendy would guiltily note to herself that she ought to do genealogical research like Sister Martin. In every Relief Society lesson or sacrament meeting talk she would find something to add to the list, not realizing how lengthy and impossible that list was growing. She scrambled and scraped to accomplish many of those things while feeling guilty and torturing herself over the ones she couldn't seem to do enough or at all. She was under stress almost constantly. When she fell short of her perception of "perfection" she would stew about it and suffer over it for days.

In fact, she not only felt guilty over what she couldn't accomplish but also felt guilty for Brent and the children when she thought they fell short of perfection as well. She was trying to drive herself and the family into the celestial kingdom like a herd of cattle!

Luckily for our family, she couldn't keep it up. Mentally, emotionally, spiritually, and physically it all came crashing down on her. Her mind and body began to shut down until she became filled with feelings of fear, panic, hopelessness, depression, and even despair. She imagined that God had deserted her, a feeling she had never experienced before. She remembers thinking, "This must be what it feels like to be in hell."

This is the point where she had to begin her re-education. Like the Prophet Joseph Smith in Liberty Jail, she found herself crying, "O God, where art thou?" And also like the Prophet, she found that before long she was comforted and taught of the Lord.

The Lord never deserts his children. Yet sometimes, like a parent teaching a toddler to walk, he steps back and holds out his arms to see if we can come to him on our own, thus enhancing our own abilities and understanding. Sometimes we must make that leap of faith and step out into the darkness, believing that at some point we will enjoy his sustaining embrace once again. If we falter, as we usually will on our own, he steps forward to catch us and enfold us in his merciful arms and put us back on our feet to try again.

Wendy had a grinding and grueling retraining ahead of her. In a manner of speaking, she had to learn to walk all over again. She had learned to run; to run faster than she had strength; to run all eight lanes of the race at once. What she didn't realize was that this was not what the Lord had required of her. She had blindly required it of herself. She had been running so fast that she never thought to stop and ask what the Lord wanted her to do. Now she couldn't even crawl. The only way she could make any progress was in letting the Savior carry her. He carried her a lot in those first few months and even years of her depression.

A month prior to Wendy's "breakdown" the Lord tried to warn her. She was editing her husband's manuscript for a book on life-long repentance, to be called *Though Your Sins Be As Scarlet*. As she thoughtfully read of and pondered on the grace and mercy that are available to *everyone* through the gift and power of Jesus Christ, the Spirit whispered to her:

3

"You are not allowing the atonement of Jesus Christ to operate in your life. You think you must do it all yourself. He wants to help and you won't let him. You are denying his atonement." She had always considered herself as one who was grateful for the gift of repentance and made use of it for more serious missteps, but she had never considered it as a principle to be applied to every step along the way.

She was receptive to the message, but old habits die slowly. As hard as Wendy tried to apply this new revelation to her life, a lifetime of intense internal and external programming kept taking over. She tried constantly to talk herself into believing she didn't have to be perfect on her own, but the old voices in her head were still shouting her down. During her pain-induced reschooling she had to learn all over again what it really means to live the gospel. The Lord taught her kindly but consistently that the kingdom of God is not found primarily in outward accomplishments and observances; "the kingdom of God is within you" (Luke 17:21).

The Cultural Gospel and the Lord's Gospel

As Wendy began to evaluate the cause of her pain and exhaustion, she realized that there are two main standards we in the Church often set up for ourselves—the Lord's standard and a social standard. One day she even began listing the Lord's commandments; and in a second column next to each one she could list the more stringent interpretation of it which had evolved in the Mormon culture. Perhaps it had come about in the same way as the well-intended

4

"fences" which had grown up around the law of Moses among the scribes and Pharisees. In order to avoid breaking any commandment, they prescribed a whole set of lesser, stricter observances which would keep them from even coming near a violation of the law or which would enable them to demonstrate a supposedly greater faithfulness than what was required in keeping a particular commandment. In their zealousness, however, they often became obsessed with the letter of these lesser laws while overlooking and sometimes offending the spirit of the original law. Worst of all, they sometimes set up such performances as the standard of righteousness, judging others unrighteously thereby. Hence, for example, their blasphemous attempt to condemn Jesus Christ for healing a man on the Sabbath (see Luke 6:7).

To a lesser extent many fall into the trap of fences today. We may be well meaning in our attempts to be "super-faithful," but when these higher standards we have created for ourselves (the Lord doesn't necessarily require them) are used to judge self and/or others unrighteously, they become stumbling blocks rather than stepping-stones.

For example, first on Wendy's list was the commandment to "multiply and replenish the earth." In our society this seems to be popularly interpreted to mean that every couple should have a *big* family. A few well-meaning members of the Church (always those who had been blessed with the ability, health, and energy to have and rear many children) had kindly pointed out Wendy and Brent's deficiency in this area. Since we had *only* four children, Wendy believed she really must have more in order to measure up, even though she already felt that she had reached her emotional capacity. She was trying to "be faithful" and conceive another baby at the time she had her "breakdown."

Another example she listed was the Word of Wisdom. A few basic health laws are laid out in the revelation recorded in section 89 of the Doctrine and Covenants, but it seems many are trying to add fences to these. Some have tried to suggest that eating white bread or refined white sugar is a violation of the Word of Wisdom. Others would add chocolate to the list of "no-nos." Cola drinks are the most notorious and controversial, but though drinking them may not be wise, it has not been defined as a sin. Yet Wendy had spent years "stressed out" over Brent's tendency to partake of this supposedly forbidden substance. Sometimes she had nagged him about it, thinking his salvation was in jeopardy and worrying that others might be led astray by his "bad" example. In so doing she disrupted the harmony of the home, and surely the greater sin was hers.

We are also commanded to serve and do our duty in the Church; to magnify our callings. In their zealousness, many have interpreted this to mean that we must never turn down any calling or ask to be released from one at any time. This was the standard Wendy felt she must measure up to when she was serving as Primary president and as the tired, stressed-out mother of three children under the age of three. Things were falling apart at home, yet she continually accepted additional assignments, thinking she must be faithful; and worst of all, she kept forgetting her new baby. Her life was so busy and stress-filled that she would forget and leave the baby at the church or other places. Moreover the baby looked as if she was newly released from a concentration camp, because Wendy seldom had time to make sure she took all the contents of her bottle. When our marriage finally began to suffer under the constant strain, Wendy prayed one night that the Lord would let the bishop know if she should be released, because she "didn't dare ask." The next day the bishop told her, "I've been feeling lately like I ought to release you." Mercifully, the Lord didn't expect her to hold on to the calling at all costs; she only *thought* he did because "others" said he did.

As Wendy made her list she realized that she had fallen into this trap with almost every commandment. She had been practicing "The Gospel According to Popular Interpretation," instead of living the gospel according to the guidance of the Holy Spirit. Ultimately it was her own fault, but she realized that in many ways traditional Mormon society (not the institutional Church itself) may also be a bit confused. President Brigham Young remonstrated with the Latter-day Saints of his day for an attitude that tended to put social pressure on others.

> How I regret the ignorance of this people—how it floods my heart with sorrow to see so many Elders of Israel who wish everybody to come to their standard and be measured by their measure. Every man must be just so long, to fit their iron bedstead, or be cut off to the right length: if too short, he must be stretched, to fill the requirement.
>
> If they see an erring brother or sister, whose course does not comport with their particular ideas of things, they conclude at once that he or she cannot be a Saint, and withdraw their fellowship, concluding that, if they are in the path of truth, others must have precisely their weight and dimensions. (*Journal of Discourses* 8:8–9.)

Generally speaking, Latter-day Saints are an obedient and sincere people. In our desire to be faithful in all things, however, we may have created a culture that at some times and in some ways unwittingly puts too much emphasis on outward conformity and in turn creates unrealistic and even false standards of "righteousness." While we must of necessity measure some things by discernible behavior, we may see that behavior as the end in itself and forget that it is the means to an end—an inner being molded into the image of Christ. In subtle and not-so-subtle ways we may be putting a lot of social pressure on one another to manifest openly measurable good works—the more measurable, the better.

Wendy came to see, for instance, that we may unintentionally hold up, as the standard to be met, our own or another's well-intended behavior rather than the Lord's gentle, steady, and compassionate guidelines and commandments. Wendy would hear (and undoubtedly make) such well-meaning statements as, "We have never missed a family home evening," "The bishop's family never watches television on Sunday," or "The prophet has said we should read the scriptures for at least half an hour each day." The list could go on. While such pronouncements were meant to commend the faithful and hold them up as examples, they inflicted wounds of discouragement on those, like Wendy and perhaps many of the rest of us, who were struggling to do their best but who might not have been able to meet such high standards—at least in that particular area. Such persons might then feel that their efforts were unacceptable.

Worst of all, as Wendy had discovered, that specific interpretation of living the commandment may not be what the Lord expects or even wants from some individuals. Loving persuasion and encouragement for even the smallest of efforts would be a better approach for motivating one another: "Try to hold regular family home evenings and don't give up if you miss once in a while." "Make an effort to keep the Sabbath day holy by following the promptings of the Spirit and doing what works best for your family." "If you can, read the scriptures for half an hour each day as the prophet has suggested, or, if not, read as you are able." These would be better ways to encourage the actions that will lead to the changed inner and outer being. We should remember the wise adage that goals (or perhaps commandments, in this case) are stars to guide us and not sticks with which to beat ourselves.

Church programs, if not administered with love, flexibility, and sensitivity, can also create rigid expectations. The inspired programs that were intended to lead her to salvation were the very things that sometimes discouraged, overwhelmed, and seemingly condemned Wendy because of their constant requirements. She forgot that people and their needs are more important than programs and their demands. When Wendy suddenly couldn't do all that was required in the auxiliary activities of the Church, there were some who questioned her faithfulness even though her heart was still as devout as ever, if not more so. They had also misunderstood the whole point of the perfecting programs of the Church.

In addition Wendy, like others, had lost sight of the fact that the Church is a purely volunteer organization. No member *has* to do anything he or she doesn't choose to do. With the exception of a few individuals employed by the Church, everything accomplished in the wards and branches of the Church is the donated gift of amateurs with varying levels of ability, commitment, and time. And yet sometimes we criticize the performance or nonperformance of our-selves and other members as if we ought to produce results unfailingly and like paid professionals, or as if we are answerable to each other rather than to God.

Finally, as leaders, parents, and others, frustrated over statistics or other outward indicators that don't seem to measure up, we may resort to motivation by guilt—repeatedly telling each other we're not doing enough. There may be many other factors, including the subtle workings and discouragement of Satan, that create the social pressure we put on ourselves and one another to conform and perform. If we are not constantly mindful, we may make that pressure greater than the steady and loving inducement to sim-ply live the true gospel of Jesus Christ according to the sweet and gentle guidance of the Holy Spirit. Elder Dallin H. Oaks warned against such a tendency in reference to genealogical work, but we suggest his counsel may be applied more generally. "Members of this church have many individual circumstances— age, health, education, place of residence, family re-sponsibilities, financial circumstances, . . . and many others. If we encourage members in this work without taking these individual circumstances into account, we may do more to impose guilt than to further the work." ("Family History: 'In Wisdom and Order,' " *Ensign,* June 1989, p. 6.)

Living the Gospel from the Inside Out

Wendy now considers herself to be one of the lucky ones. Though it is knowledge born of pain, the truths she learned because of her depression have set her free from the misunderstanding of "religion" that once hindered her from finding the real meaning and purpose of the gospel of Jesus Christ. Deep pain has become deeper joy.

At one time during his ministry the outward-looking Pharisees demanded to know of Christ "when the kingdom of God should come." He replied: "The kingdom of God cometh not with observation: neither shall they say, Lo here! or, lo there! For behold, the kingdom of God is within you." (Luke 17:20–21.) The Joseph Smith Translation clarifies this with the wording, "the kingdom of God has already come unto you." Elder Bruce R. McConkie explains this to mean, "The Church and kingdom has already been organized; it is here." He comments further that "men have the inherent capacity to gain salvation in the celestial world; in a sense this power is within them; and so it might be said that the kingdom of God is within a person" inasmuch as he will obey the gospel's laws and ordinances. (See *Doctrinal New Testament Commentary*, 3 vols. [Salt Lake City: Bookcraft, 1965–73], 1:540.) Apparently, then, the Savior was teaching these spiritually myopic Pharisees that one cannot find the kingdom of God simply by looking for it externally, because if he or she does not carry it *within* it will not be recognizable *without*.

The kingdom of God is a gathering of people who are pledged to that kingdom and carry its principles within themselves. Though we may participate and live in the midst of the Church and Mormon society, if the kingdom of God is not thus *within* us we do not truly belong to it. On the other hand, if we genuinely carry it within we are part of the kingdom regardless of the superfluous, cultural standards others may set for membership. President David O. McKay cautioned against a type of looking outward for the kingdom of God in our own lives. "Mere compliance with the word of the Lord, without a corresponding inward desire, will avail but little. Indeed, such outward actions and pretending phrases may disclose hypocrisy, a sin that Jesus most vehemently condemned." (As quoted in Dallin H. Oaks, *Pure in Heart* [Salt Lake City: Bookcraft, 1988], p. 33.)

How do we internalize the kingdom of God so that the outward observances arise from the inward desires? Wendy discovered that one of the most liberating and joyful things a person can learn to do is to stop trying so hard to please other people—stop caring so much what they say or what they think—and simply try to please the Lord. Anne Morrow Lindbergh, in her thoughtful book, *Gift from the Sea,* acknowledged that "the most exhausting thing in life, . . . is being insincere" (New York: Vintage Books, 1978, p. 32). We are not talking here about the blatant hypocrisy mentioned above or deliberate attempts to deceive others. We are talking about well-meaning attempts to try to be what we think others think we should be or to live up to some imagined but mistaken and impossible ideal. It takes integrity and humility to be what one is, not caught up in appearances. It takes courage to do what the Lord wants us to do, or not do, when it doesn't fit the *social* perception of a "faithful" or "active" Latter-day Saint. It boils down to continually seeking and following the guidance of the Spirit, not "fearing men more than God" (see D&C 3:7).

When Wendy could no longer "do it all" (in fact, she could hardly do anything), she had to depend on the Lord in order just to accomplish the simplest things. That was the great blessing which came not only to her but also to our entire family. We learned from our own painful experience the meaning of what the Lord taught Moroni: that he doesn't *expect* us to be perfect in this life. He expects us to do all we can but knows we won't be able to "do it all." He desires that our shortcomings will cause us to turn to him, so that out of our weaknesses he can make strengths. "And if men come unto me I will show unto them their weakness. I give unto men weakness that they may be humble; and my grace is sufficient for all men that humble themselves before me; for if they humble themselves before me, and have faith in me, then will I make weak things become strong unto them" (Ether 12:27).

Thus Wendy's weakness and subsequent depression brought her to her knees, to depending on the Lord for help just to get out of bed in the morning, clean her home, and feed her family. For that reason she had to consult the Lord, to seek his Spirit, and to follow his guidance. And whatever he wanted her to do, he gave her strength to do. In addition to soliciting his will, she learned to prayerfully assess her own abilities and resources—to be diligent, constant, and steady, but not to run faster than she had strength. Best of all, she discovered that the rewards of doing the Lord's will are far greater than the rewards of social approval.

Wendy has come to delight in the satisfaction of doing the right things for the right reasons, of giving of herself because she wants to and feels inspired to, of living the joyous gospel of Jesus Christ from the heart. It is such a wonderful and fulfilling way to live and it almost seems like a luxury, because she was so used to forcing herself to perform when her heart wasn't in it. She can say no without being deluged in a flood of guilt but bathed in the confirming warmth of the Spirit instead. Ironically, the more of her own "super-faithfulness" she eliminates, the more truly full of faith in the Lord she becomes and the greater her capacity to render meaningful service. That elusive feeling of self-worth and inner peace came not from *what she could do,* but from *what the Lord can do with her.*

In his earthly ministry the Savior tried to teach us to live by this principle: "Abide in me, and I in you. As the branch cannot bear fruit of itself, except it abide in the vine; no more can ye, except ye abide in me. I am the vine, ye are the branches: He that abideth in me, and I in him, the same bringeth forth much fruit: for without me ye can do nothing." (John 15:4–5.)

Unfortunately, many Church members still seem to be caught up in the exhausting trap of the "cultural gospel." They are almost completely missing the point of the true gospel—the "peaceable things—that which bringeth joy, that which bringeth life eternal" (D&C 42:61). Thus the remainder of this book will be our attempt to share the truths we have learned, in hopes of sparing others the long and painful learning process we have experienced. We have tried to include some helpful thoughts and practical ideas, but in the end it all comes down to stilling the voice of one's own pride, fear, needs, desires, expectations, and willful opinions and submitting constantly and continuously to the will of the Lord.

Chapter Two

"Quiet, Sane Living"

Balancing the Temporal Demands of Today's Stress-Filled Society

*S*everal years ago, while on a family vacation, our family encountered some problems with our car. With the engine sputtering and stalling we limped into a gas station, fcarful that our vacation would have to be cut short by a long and expensive car repair. Great was our relief when the mechanic informed us that the car problem was nothing serious and all that was needed was a minor adjustment to the carburetor that would allow for a more balanced mix of gas and oxygen.

In the years since then we have had many opportunities to see how important a proper balance is not only to machinery maintenance but also in our own lives. Sometimes a minor adjustment or fine-tuning will keep our lives running smoothly. At other times, however, major repairs with their accompanying cost and inconvenience are required because we have allowed our lives to be out of balance too long. Expensive tires have to be completely replaced, not just rotated or repaired, when they have been driven too long in an unbalanced condition. Engines often require major repairs when owners pay little attention to the imperative need for regular oil changes. Likewise we need to frequently check the balance of our lives. A periodic tune-up of our personal priorities and a regular safety inspection of the direction and desired destination of our lives helps to insure us against major temporal, emotional, and spiritual breakdowns.

Elder M. Russell Ballard of the Quorum of the Twelve reflected on his own serious illness and how it helped him to take inventory of his life and conduct a personal balance check. From his own experience he was then able to compassionately counsel members of the Church.

> The night before my surgery, my doctors talked about the possibility of cancer. When I was left alone, my mind filled with thoughts of my family and of my ministry. I found comfort in the ordinances of the gospel that bind me to my family if we are faithful. I realized that I needed to rearrange some of my priorities to accomplish the things that matter most to me.
>
> Sometimes we need a personal crisis to reinforce in our minds what we really value and cherish. . . . Perhaps if you, too, search your hearts and courageously assess the priorities of your life, you may discover, as I did, that you need a better balance among your priorities. ("Keeping Life's Demands in Balance," *Ensign,* May 1987, p. 13.)

Keeping the daily demands of life in balance is one of the great juggling acts of mortality. All of us, though at different times and in different ways, feel pulled and tugged in different directions. Even trying to do good and faithfully live gospel principles, especially amidst the challenges and complexities of modern society, can be carried to extremes and upset the delicate balance of our lives, painfully intruding upon our personal peace and family harmony. In an address to a women's conference at BYU, Sister Norma B. Ashton, wife of Elder Marvin J. Ashton of the Quorum of the Twelve, spoke eloquently of the need for balance in one's life. " 'Patty Perfect' has had a lot of publicity, and she has fallen from favor lately," quipped Sister Ashton. "She is the woman who seems to be able to do everything well but then has a nervous breakdown caused by guilt feelings because she isn't doing enough." ("A Unique Melody," *Ensign,* September 1989, p. 24.)

This pointed observation struck a particularly personal and painful chord for our family. As detailed in chapter 1, Wendy experienced this "Patty Perfect syndrome" that Sister Ashton described. During his years of service as a bishop and in other leadership callings Brent discovered that Wendy's experience was not unique. In fact, he found that discouragement, depression, and the stress-induced problems resulting from a life out of balance was probably the most common problem he encountered among members of his ward. Being stressed out, pulled in every direction, and feeling hopelessly unable to do all that is expected, can sap us of inward spiritual strength and leave us unhappy, unfulfilled, and even bitter. In this weakened condition we may become more vulnerable to the "fiery darts of the adversary," and other temptations and problems may wedge their way into our lives. This is not unique to the Top family, our friends, or the faithful members of our own ward, but is a problem facing the Church generally and is increasing continually. Elder Dean L. Larsen, of the Seventy, has observed:

> I seem to be encountering more and more frequently in my circulation among the membership of the Church, people who are honestly trying to avoid sin, who are really doing their best, as they understand, to live in accordance with the principles of the gospel but who are unhappy, frustrated, and disillusioned to a considerable degree. Let me use extractions from several letters that have come to me from such people to illustrate the nature of the problem to which I refer:
>
> > "Please understand, we are trying. We know that these are the last days, and so much needs to be done. We do not want to be numbered among the inactives, but for the first time it is beginning to look better and better."
>
> Have you ever run into people like that? Here is another:
>
> > "Is it really a matter of piling it on to see how much one can take? A survival of the fittest? I can't imagine Heavenly Father wanting it to be this way."
>
> There is some anguish in that serious question. . . . Here is another:
>
> > "Life has ceased to have any meaning. . . . I cannot see any way out except to quit. I just wish I could walk away from all of it—sometimes from everything."
>
> There is some desperation expressed here—in the life of one who is obviously a member trying to do what is right. . . . Now, this is not an isolated reaction. I don't think that is an isolated feeling or condition

among our own people today, and I believe sincerely it is one of the significant challenges that you and I and those with whom we are associated are going to have to deal with in this stressful, challenging time. (Dean L. Larsen, Address given to the Association of Mormon Counselors and Psychotherapists, October 2, 1986, pp. 6, 8; copy in possession of author.)

To be able to receive the abundance of life that the Lord has promised (see John 10:10) we must make room to receive it by vigilantly preserving the temporal and spiritual balance of our lives. "Striking the proper balance is one of the keenest tests of our agency," observed Elder Neal A. Maxwell. "Therefore, we need to ask regularly for inspiration in the use of our time and in the making of our daily decisions." (*Notwithstanding My Weakness* [Salt Lake City: Deseret Book Co., 1981], p. 5.)

The English poet William Wordsworth penned in the early nineteenth century his classic poem, "The World Is Too Much with Us." His insightful observation of his own society certainly remains relevant to us today as we seek to balance the many challenges and demands placed upon us by modern society.

> The world is too much with us; late and soon,
> Getting and spending, we lay waste our powers:
> Little we see in Nature that is ours;
> We have given our hearts away, a sordid boon!

The imbalance between the temporal and spiritual life is an age-old problem which seems to be snowballing under the fast pace and stresses of modern society. We "give our hearts away" and in turn "we lay waste our powers" in a variety of ways.

The Materialism Mirage

The avalanche of materialism with all its glittering enticements threatens to sweep us away and bury us alive. Observed Elder M. Russell Ballard, "Perhaps none need the principle of balance in their lives more than those who are driven toward accumulating 'things' in this world" ("Keeping Life's Demands in Balance," p. 14). Prophets of God, both ancient and modern, have consistently warned against setting our hearts upon the things of the world. The Apostle Paul declared, "The love of money is the root of all evil" (1 Timothy 6:10). Neither money nor the material things that money can buy are in and of themselves inherently evil, but the desire for money and the things of the world is the root of evil in that it can become a driving force in our lives—so compelling and powerful that it may distract us and divert us from the things of God. The Savior on several occasions portrayed wealth and materialism as a potential stumbling block to true discipleship (see Mark 10:17–25; Matthew 6:24) and of little enduring value. "Take heed, and beware of covetousness," he admonished his disciples, "for a man's life consisteth not in the abundance of the things which he posesseth"

> And he spake a parable unto them, saying, The ground of a certain rich man brought forth plentifully:
> And he thought within himself, saying, What shall I do, because I have no room where to bestow my fruits?
> And he said, This will I do: I will pull down my barns, and build greater; and there will I bestow all my fruits and goods.
> And I will say to my soul, Soul, thou hast much goods laid up for many years; take thine ease, eat, drink, and be merry.

But God said unto him, Thou fool, this night thy soul shall be required of thee: then whose shall those things be, which thou hast provided?

So is he that layeth up treasure for himself, and is not rich toward God. (Luke 12:15–21.)

The scriptures command us to work by the sweat of the brow to provide the basic necessities for ourselves and our families. We also speak about the "just wants" that we may have. Both terms—"basic necessities" and "just wants"—are relative. What we in the United States may consider "basic necessities," to some people in some parts of the world would be considered luxurious, opulent, or even excessive. All too often in this day and age when we speak of our "just wants" it really is a means of saying "I *just want* this and I *just want* that." This modern trap of materialism has the potential to ensnare all of us if we are not vigilant—if we are not seeking to root out of our lives those materialistic trends and temptations that may sidetrack us from our eternal objectives. With eyes single to the glory of God we need to be constantly seeking *first* the kingdom of God (see Jacob 2:13–19).

In our day the Lord's anointed prophet President Ezra Taft Benson likewise warned the Latter-day Saints: "Do not be caught up in materialism, one of the real plagues of our generation" ("To the Single Adult Brethren of the Church," *Ensign,* May 1988, p. 53).

We often think of materialism as a forerunner to pride. Prophets both ancient and modern have warned us concerning the pitfalls of pride. Being materialistic is dangerous not only because it often leads to pride and selfishness and the myriad other sins and temptations that accompany the things of the world but also because it may divert us from other more meaningful contributions and service. In response to the Savior's warning that it is easier for a camel to go through the eye of a needle than for a rich man to enter heaven (see Matthew 19:24) some of us seem to say, "I'll take my chances!" We want to show the Lord that we are the exceptions to the rule—that we can indeed somehow serve God and mammon simultaneously. "Bless me with riches and I'll show you I can still be humble," we might boast. Elder Joseph B. Wirthlin warned against the diversions and distractions of materialism.

> Even though the teachings of the Savior are plain and direct, we are still at risk of getting sidetracked. Some people choose to follow the teachings of the Lord and of his living prophet only when convenient, but reject them when sacrifice or deeper commitment is required. Some fail to follow only because His divine teachings do not agree with their own preconceived notions.

> We get sidetracked by submitting to temptations that divert us past the bounds of safety. Satan knows our weaknesses. He puts attractive snares on our paths at just those moments when we are most vulnerable. His intent is to lead us from the way that returns us to our Heavenly Father. Sin may result from activities that begin innocently or that are perfectly legitimate in moderation, but in excess, they can cause us to veer from the straight and narrow path to our destruction. . . .

> [One] temptation to detour us is placing improper emphasis on the obtaining of material possessions. For example, we may build a beautiful, spacious home that is far larger than we need. We may spend far too much to decorate, furnish, and landscape it. And even if we are blessed enough to afford such luxury, we may be misdirecting resources that could be better used to build the kingdom of God or to feed and clothe our needy brothers and sisters. ("The Straight and Narrow Way," *Ensign*, November 1990, p. 65.)

We (Wendy and Brent) discovered in our own lives, exactly as Elder Wirthlin described, how seeking after the things of the world, even when done innocently, can snowball into an avalanche that threatens personal peace and financial stability. We have never made a lot of money and have always scrimped and saved for what we got. Finances have always seemed tight, and we have made conscientious efforts to avoid the alluring "fast track" and "high life" of modern society. But unfortunately we have felt the ever-tightening tentacles of materialism grab at our family. We did not seek this temptation. In fact, we had through the years purposely sought to avoid it. Nevertheless we came to experience an ever-so-subtle shift in our priorities and an adjustment of our view of what constituted basic necessities and just wants. It was when we built a new house that we came face to face with the plague of materialism and found ourselves feeling and thinking things that not only surprised us but also forced us to reevaluate our priorities and rebalance the temporal part of our lives.

After the house was built we found ourselves dissatisfied with the old furniture, so we set about acquiring new furniture. One early purchase was a new entertainment center—hence we became dissatisfied with the old stereo; we needed to get out of the "dark ages" of records and buy a compact disc player. When we had obtained a new CD player, of course, we had to start buying CDs. It all seemed so logical and justifiable. We soon found that after every new purchase we were faced with numerous other attractive items that appeared so necessary and justifiable. It was a never-ending cycle—the more we acquired, the more we felt we needed.

Instead of feeling happiness with our new home, feeling grateful for the blessings of the Lord in our lives and a contentment with what we had (which was more than previously we had ever thought we would have), we instead felt frustrated at not being able to have all we wanted. Instead of having a spirit of peace and harmony in our home, a spirit of worship and gratitude, we found ourselves using our time and energies in fretting about draperies and landscaping, and worrying about whether we would be able to afford what we wanted and how we were going to pay for the things we had purchased.

This experience opened our eyes to the ease with which we can lay waste our powers—spiritual and emotional, as well as financial—when we even unwittingly become sidetracked from the pursuit of eternal treasures and turn our primary attention to the transitory things of the world. We learned that the many manifestations of materialism are like a mirage: We see something desirable and work our way to that objective, only to find that when we reach it we are not fulfilled and contented but rather are frustrated that "all we ever wanted" in a material sense is never enough.

Seeking the things of the world leaves a person always feeling that he has never quite arrived. There will always be mirages that appear and disappear before us in our trek through life. Chasing after the mirage of materialism wastes our time, saps us of our energy, and inevitably leaves us spiritually and emotionally empty. Although the following words of Isaiah were being used in a different doctrinal context, the image he creates can also apply to those of us who periodically find themselves in the modern maze of materialism—like the hamster in the wheel running in circles but never reaching the desired destination—seeking happiness and personal fulfillment in material things, only to find that enduring fulfillment is not found in things. "It shall be unto them, even as unto a hungry man which dreameth, and behold he eateth but he awaketh and his soul is empty; or like unto a thirsty man which dreameth, and behold he drinketh but he awaketh and behold he is faint, and his soul hath appetite" (2 Nephi 27:3).

When we allow the world to be too much with us and find that most of our time and effort is consumed in getting and spending, whether done innocently in the pursuit of noble causes or knowingly in selfish service of mammon, we give our hearts away. Without the necessary balance of temporal things in our lives, we may get and spend only to discover that we have actually laid waste our emotional and spiritual strength and given our hearts away to things that matter very little in the end. Isaiah, as quoted by the Book of Mormon prophet Jacob, warned, "Do not spend money for that which is of no worth, nor your labor for that which cannot satisfy" (2 Nephi 9:51). Perhaps each of us needs to carefully take inventory not only of our earthly and eternal priorities but also of how we are actually spending our time, talents, and resources. Are we seeking first and foremost for a lasting legacy of love and righteousness for our families, or are we just leaving them *things* that, like old Christmas toys, wear out, lose their appeal, and are abandoned in closets and attics?

Day-Planner Syndrome

Another way in which the world is too much with us is how we spend our time and expend our energies. "We give our lives," observed Elder William R.

Bradford, "to that which we give our time" ("Unclutter Your Life," *Ensign*, May 1992, p. 28). Just as getting and spending may lay waste our financial, emotional, and spiritual powers and disturb inward stillness, so also can all the "coming and going" and "hurrying and scurrying" of today's world.

More than two thousand years ago King Benjamin had to warn his people about going to unbalanced extremes, even in doing good for others, and this ancient counsel certainly has relevance to the emotional and spiritual challenges of our day. After expounding the many requirements for gospel living, he cautioned: "And see that all these things are done in wisdom and order; for it is not requisite that a man should run faster than he has strength. And again, it is expedient that he should be diligent, that thereby he might win the prize; therefore, all things must be done in order." (Mosiah 4:27.) It is one of the great temptations of today's society to "run faster than [we have] strength." Sometimes we are led to believe that in order to be successful in life we must run faster, work harder, and produce more than the next person. Even the positive traits of being goal or achievement oriented can be taken too far when we neglect the charge to "see that all these things are done in wisdom and order."

We commonly encounter people who have succumbed to what may be characterized as day-planner syndrome. Their lives are so planned and structured and stretched to the limits that there is no room for the things that matter most—that which the Lord would have them do. "We go around in circles," observed Elder Robert L. Simpson, "and we spend our time in triviality when we should get on with that which the Lord has given us to do by way of foreordination" ("Cast Your Burden Upon the Lord," *Speeches of the Year*, 1974 [Provo: Brigham Young University Press, 1975], p. 61). Just as we may unwisely overschedule ourselves with a day planner to the point that we have no time for personal rejuvenation or other imperative matters, so too we will lose out on significant spiritual gifts, as well as emotional strength, if we disrupt the delicate balance in our lives. Paraphrasing St. Augustine, C. S. Lewis wrote: "God wants to give us something, but cannot, because our hands are full—there's nowhere for Him to put it" (*The Problem of Pain* [New York: Macmillan, 1962], p. 96). In our day, President Spencer W. Kimball prophetically urged the Saints to return to what he characterized as "quiet, sane living" (*Faith Precedes the Miracle* [Salt Lake City: Deseret Book Co., 1972], p. 265).

In striking the temporal balance of our time, we are often forced to make hard choices between many good and desirable things. For example, providing varied educational and cultural experiences for our children is valuable in helping develop talents and promoting personal growth. Being involved in Church service or community affairs also may provide us with rich and rewarding experiences as individuals. But we need to follow the counsel of Elder M. Russell Ballard: "Remember, too much of anything in life can throw us off balance. At the same time, too little of the important things can do the same thing." ("Keeping Life's Demands in Balance," p. 16.) It may be that the worst thing we can give our children is an *additional* sports camp, music lesson, or other type of activity that demands money and time away from the family. "They do not need everything the neighbor's children across the street are receiving," Elder L. Tom Perry observed. "Of course, we want them to develop their talents, but do they need to enroll in every athletic camp or every cultural development course which comes along?" ("Train Up a Child," *Ensign,* November 1988, p. 74.) Teaching our children to live a quiet, sane, and balanced life is one of the most important parental tasks of our day.

As parents, members, and leaders in the Church, it is easy to feel that we need to be continually serving, leading, or counselling in order to magnify our callings. As important as each of these types of service is to Church and family, it may sometimes be that we render more significant service and develop more substantive spirituality by having less meetings and activities. "Sometimes more can be less, and sometimes less is more," stated Elder Boyd K. Packer ("Teach Them Correct Principles," *Ensign,* May 1990, p. 90). There is an essential balance that must be struck between being "anxiously engaged in a good cause" (D&C 58:27) and being so over-involved in *so many* "good causes" that we are drawn away from things that matter most. Our lives are out of balance if we allow outward busyness to supplant inner goodness. Elder Neal A. Maxwell counselled: "So often our hardest choices are between competing and desirable alternatives (each with righteous consequences), when there is *not* time to do both at once. Indeed, it is at the mortal intersections—where time and talent and opportunities meet—that priorities, like traffic lights, are sorely needed. Quiet sustained goodness is the order of heaven, not conspicuous but episodic busyness." (*Notwithstanding My Weakness,* p. 5.)

Putting First Things First

There are many people in the world who come to the end of their mortal existence and sadly discover that they have in essence given away precious parts of their lives by giving their time and attention to things that really mattered little. Eternal priorities absolutely must guide our lives and actions, for without them we will end up spending our time and resources on terrestial things to the exclusion of things of a celestial quality. "We need to examine all the ways we use our time: our work, our ambitions, our affiliations, and the habits that drive our actions," urged Elder William R. Bradford.

As we make such a study, we will be able to better understand what we should really be spending our time doing.

At the top of our list of basics, we will surely have the family. Next only to our devotion to God, the family comes first. Their temporal and spiritual well-being is of vital importance, and so there must be work to provide for it. This means hard work. . . .

A mother should never allow herself to become so involved with extras that she finds herself neglecting her divine role. A father must not let any activity, no matter how interesting or important it may seem, keep him from giving of himself in the one-on-one service and close, constant care of each member of the family.

The titles of Mother and Father will persist after this life. All that we may acquire and any titles we may earn which are worldly will pass away. In the meantime, they may be cluttering up our lives and affecting our eternal outcome.

Young people must learn that none of the exciting and entertaining and fun things are worth it if they

29

take you off from the path that will lead you back home to your Heavenly Father. ("Unclutter Your Life," p. 28.)

This principle has been consistently taught by leaders of the Church through inspired counsel as well as in necessary course corrections for the Church. The consolidated meeting schedule and the revised budget policy are but two examples of how the Church and its leaders are urging us to return to "quiet, sane living" and expend our energy and our resources on those things that will have ultimate, eternal significance. Just as these principles apply to the institutional Church, so do they apply to individual homes and families. "The primary responsibility for building testimonies and providing faith-building experiences in our members, including our youth, resides in the home," declared President Thomas S. Monson. "The Church should continue to support the determination of the family to do this." ("The Lord's Way," *Ensign,* May 1990, p. 93.)

The change that has been made in the budgeting policy is an example of an inspired course correction that, as Elder Boyd K. Packer stated, "will have the effect of returning much of the responsibility for teaching and counseling and activity to the family where it belongs. . . . There will be fewer intrusions into family schedules and in the family purses. Church activities must be replaced by family activities." ("Teach Them Correct Principles," p. 90.) We should recognize that if the prophets have made adjustments to major Church programs and policies to draw the Saints home to their primary responsibilities, we should take inventory of our own temporal balance—both time and money spent—and make the necessary coinciding adjustments in our lives.

We must not look beyond the mark (see Jacob 4:14) by assuming that being anxiously engaged in *any* good cause will produce blessings equal to those resulting from work in any other good cause. In today's hectic, fast-paced society, it may be that the "good cause" we should anxiously engage ourselves in is to become less busy in things of secondary significance and more devoted to relationships and works of eternal import.

It is imperative to personal peace and family harmony that we recognize that even our service in the Church should never become a means of neglecting our more eternal personal and family responsibilities. When President McKay said "no other success can compensate for failure in the home," surely that included being successful as bishops, Relief Society presidents, high councilors, teachers, advisors, or any other Church calling. In fact, we cannot truly be "successful" in any lasting and significant way in our Church service if we fail to understand eternal priorities and thus do not take care of our own family's spiritual and emotional welfare.

When we (Wendy and Brent) lived in Arizona we often heard our then Regional Representative, Elder J. Ballard Washburn, who is now a member of the Seventy, say, "Satan doesn't care whether you are in the bar or the bishop's office if he can get you to neglect your family." This has been a guiding principle in our lives. The longer we serve in the Church the more convinced we become that what is needed in the Church today is not more dynamic leaders, more effective programs, or more activities, but stronger families. Part of achieving temporal balance in our lives consists in removing from our schedules matters of secondary significance that may actually interfere with or impede our eternal priorities. The Church, with all of its programs and activities, is a resource for families and must never become a substitute for, or even a roadblock to, the eternal family unit.

"Salvation is a family affair," observed Elder Bruce R. McConkie. President Harold B. Lee taught priesthood leaders that more emphasis needed to be placed on creating strong families and less on Church programs.

> The home is the basis of a righteous life. With new and badly needed emphasis on the "how," [of Church programs] we must not lose sight of the "why" we are so engaged. The priesthood programs operate in support of the home; the auxiliary programs render valuable assistance. . . . Both the revelations of God and the learning of men tell us how crucial the home is in shaping the individual's total life experience. . . . Much of what we do [in the Church] organizationally, then, is scaffolding, as we seek to build the individual, and we must not mistake the scaffolding for the soul. (Conference Report, October 1967, p. 107.)

Other General Authorities also have referred to this "scaffolding concept"—that Church programs and activities are only the means to an end, not the end in and of themselves. Elder Neal A. Maxwell counselled the Saints, "Let us not mistake program scaffolding for substance" ("Be of Good Cheer," *Ensign,* November 1982, p. 68). The man and woman of Christ, who have inward stillness, recognize that "some Church aids are, in a sense, scaffolding for the soul," as Elder Maxwell has described, "which scaffolding one day will be removed—like waterwings or training wheels." ("True Believers in Christ," *1980 Devotional Speeches of the Year* [Provo: Brigham Young University Press, 1981], p. 139.)

The Need for Personal Rejuvenation

Sometimes we fail to pull back from many of the demands placed upon our time because we are afraid such an action might be perceived as selfish on our part. But putting first things first requires that we must also preserve and protect our own spiritual, physical, and emotional health. "Do not run faster or labor more than you have strength and means," the Lord declared to the Prophet Joseph (D&C 10:4). It is difficult to build the kingdom of God, lift and serve others, and give of ourselves to those who need us if we are "burned out" or "sapped" of all spiritual, physical, and emotional strength. Like a sponge that is drained dry, we too must replenish our souls so we will have something to offer to others. "Jesus, our exemplar, often 'withdrew himself into the wilderness, and prayed'" (Luke 5:16), said Elder M. Russell Ballard. "We need to do the same thing occasionally to rejuvenate ourselves spiritually as the Savior did." ("Keeping Life's Demands in Balance," p. 14). Perhaps sometimes we can best rejuvenate and strengthen ourselves and our families by withdrawing from the pressing demands of life. To preserve the temporal balance of our lives we may need to say no to extra projects, personal or professional pursuits, social activities, and other invitations for which we do not have the time, resources, or energies. We need not feel guilty or selfish in pulling back to regroup in this way, for there is a strength that comes from sometimes just being home with "no place to go." Edgar A. Guest wrote:

> The happiest nights I ever know
> Are those when I have No place to go,
> And the missus says when the day is through:

"Tonight we haven't a thing to do."
Oh, the joy of it, and the peace untold
Of sitting 'round in my slippers old,
With my pipe and book in my easy chair,
Knowing I needn't go anywhere.
Needn't hurry my evening meal
Nor force the smiles that I do not feel,
But can grab a book from a nearby shelf,
And drop all sham and be myself.
Oh, the charm of it and the comfort rare;
Nothing on earth with it can compare;
And I'm sorry for him who doesn't know
The joy of having No place to go.

As we seek to balance the demands for our time and attention, as we are forced to make hard decisions or sacrifice activities or service that may be important but not imperative, we will come to recognize that we have lost nothing essential but rather have gained in terms of rediscovering inner peace. If we don't come to recognize this, the very things that we desire most for ourselves and our children will elude us in our getting and spending and in our often frantic, frustrated pursuit to meet all the world's demands on us.

In the Twenty-third Psalm David poetically and profoundly taught that the Savior, as the Good Shepherd, "maketh me to lie down in green pastures: he leadeth beside the still waters. He restoreth my soul." This promised restoration will bring peace in times of stress, enrichment to our lives, and renewed spiritual strength. To obtain it, however, we must be willing to walk "beside the still waters" by returning to quiet, sane living; unloading our hands and hearts of the unnecessary things of the world; reducing our "day-planner mindset"; and slowing down so we can hear the still, small voice.

Slow me down, Lord!
Ease the pounding of my heart
By the quieting of my mind.
Steady my hurried pace
With a vision of eternal reach of time.
Give me,
Amidst the confusion of my day,
The calmness of the everlasting hills.
Break the tensions of my nerves
With the soothing music of the singing streams
That live in my memory.
Help me to know
The magical restoring power of sleep.
Teach me the art
Of taking minute vacations of slowing down
   to look at a flower;
   to chat with an old friend or make a new one;
   to pet a stray dog;
   to watch a spider build a web;
   to smile at a child;
   or to read a few lines from a good book.
Remind me each day
That the race is not always to the swift;
That there is more to life than increasing its speed.
Let me look upward
Into the branches of the towering oak
And know that it grew great and strong
Because it grew slowly and well.
Slow me down, Lord,
And inspire me to send my roots deep

Into the soil of life's enduring values
That I may grow toward the stars
Of my greater destiny.
(Orin L. Crain, as quoted by Dean L. Larsen in "The
Peaceable Things of the Kingdom," *Brigham Young
University 1984–85 Devotional and Fireside Speeches*
[Provo: University Publications, 1985], pp. 71–72.)

Chapter Three

Rely upon the Mercy of Christ

Escaping the Quicksands of Perfectionism

*W*hen we (Wendy and Brent) were children the popular adventure movies and television programs included westerns and pirate stories. Like most normal children, we enjoyed going to the adventure movies on Saturdays or watching episodes of Roy Rogers or Bonanza on TV. One interesting thing we remember from episodes of those old adventures is an encounter (usually by one of the heroes in the story) with dangerous quicksands. We had never seen or encountered quicksands in our lives, but we assumed they were real. We would worry with the hero and wonder how he could escape from the dreaded quicksands. Quicksand is a mixture of sand and water that cannot support heavy weight. Since it is not completely liquid, swimming in it is impossible; and it is not completely solid, so one cannot stand on it or walk out of it. One of the characteristics of quicksand that make it so hazardous is that a person who is trapped in it sinks faster and deeper the more he tries to escape from the sandy bog.

Almost as if in quicksand, sometimes we can become bogged down with discouragement and frustration through demands and expectations related to spiritual aspects of life. Unrealistic expectations and overwhelming feelings of inadequacy can disrupt our inward peace and derail our personal pursuit of perfection. These feelings of helplessness, hopelessness, discouragement, and failure are symptoms of a life that is lacking spiritual balance. Just as the temporal imbalances of time and money demands can affect our emotional and spiritual peace, so can spiritual imbalance have a detrimental effect on every aspect of our lives and our relationships. It may not be visible like quicksand, but it is real nonetheless and can destroy us if we are left alone to flail helplessly in it. Elder Dean L. Larsen identified emotional and spiritual "burnout" as one of the destructive by-products of spiritual imbalance.

> Some of us create such a complexity of expectations for ourselves that it is difficult to cope with the magnitude of them. Sometimes we establish so many particulars by which to evaluate and rate ourselves that it becomes difficult to feel successful and worthy to any degree at any time. We can drive ourselves unmercifully toward perfection on such a broad plane. When this compulsion is intensified by sources outside ourselves, the problem is compounded. Confronting these demands can bring mental and emotional despair.

Everyone needs to feel successful and worthy in some ways at least part of the time. The recognition of our frailties need not propel us to try to achieve perfection in one dramatic commitment of effort. The best progress sometimes comes when we are not under intense duress. Overzealousness is at least as much to be feared as apathy. Trying to measure up to too many particular expectations without some sense of self-tolerance can cause spiritual and emotional "burnout." . . .

. . . In responding to these expectations, we must successfully evaluate between fundamentally important values and the sometimes superficial or outward performances that others may expect from us. ("The Peaceable Things of the Kingdom," *Brigham Young University 1984–85 Devotional and Fireside Speeches* [Provo: University Publications, 1985], pp. 72, 74.)

Much of the frustration and discouragement that comes from a life out of spiritual balance results from a misunderstanding of the doctrine of perfection and/or from a lack of faith in the grace and love of the Savior. Too often when we read the Savior's charge "Be ye therefore perfect, even as your Father which is in heaven is perfect" (Matthew 5:48) we think this means we should be perfect in every aspect of our lives—right now. Such a narrow, literalistic view of this scripture can create a spiritual form of quicksand. When we misunderstand the doctrine of becoming perfect and assume that we ought to be perfect now—without sin, never making mistakes, and always doing the ideal in every situation or in every calling— we are like one in quicksand who, the more he attempts to extricate himself by his sole efforts, the more he is actually sinking dangerously deeper. To escape the quicksands of perfectionism and to save our spiritual lives we must correctly understand what the Savior expects of us and how we can become perfect. And to maintain a sense of spiritual balance in our lives it is imperative that we recognize that neither the Savior nor modern prophets have taught that the Lord requires us to achieve perfection while in mortality.

It is helpful to know that the word *perfect* is used in the Bible in more than one sense. Two Hebrew words are used in the Old Testament text for the word that is translated as *perfect* in the King James Version of the Bible. Having a "perfect heart" is spoken of (see 1 Kings 8:61; 15:14; 2 Kings 20:3). The Hebrew word in this context is *shalem,* which means "finished" or "whole." (It is interesting to note that *shalem* shares the same root as *shalom,* which means "peace." This seems to indicate that one with a "perfect heart" would be one who enjoys an inner peace and spiritual wholeness that comes from a relationship with God.) The Lord commanded Abraham, "Walk before me, and be thou perfect" (Genesis 17:1). The Hebrew word translated as *perfect* in this context is *tammim,* which means "complete," "upright," and "undefiled." The New Testament text uses a Greek term that the KJV translates as *perfect—teleios* (see below), which, "meaning 'perfect,' also means 'complete, whole, fully initiated, mature'" (see *Encyclopedia of Mormonism* [New York: Macmillan, 1992], 3:1074; see also 2 Timothy 3:17; Matthew 5:48; 19:21; Ephesians 4:13; James 3:2).

It is clear from the above words and phrases that the term *perfect,* as used in our Bible, does not exclusively mean what we traditionally have used it to mean—without sin, or making no mistakes, or never falling short. Often the biblical emphasis is on the completion of man. We understand what is meant by perfection being the end product of man as we examine two companion statements of the Savior—one in the New Testament and the other in the Book of Mormon. Elder Russell M. Nelson explained:

> In the Sermon on the Mount [the Savior] taught his disciples, "Be ye therefore perfect, even as your Father which is in heaven is perfect" (Matthew 5:48). . . .
>
> To his disciples in the Western Hemisphere, the resurrected Lord proclaimed this divine injunction: "I would that ye should be perfect even as I, or your Father who is in heaven is perfect" (3 Nephi 12:48).
>
> How do we explain these similar but meaningfully different statements? Between the time of his Sermon on the Mount and his sermon to the Nephites, the sinless Savior had become perfected by his atonement. *Perfect* comes from the Greek word *teleios,* which connotes "to set out for a definite point or goal." It conveys the concept of conclusion of an act. Therefore, *perfect* in Matthew 5:48 also means "finished," "completed," "consummated," or "fully developed," and refers to the reality of the glorious resurrection of our Master. (*The Power Within Us* [Salt Lake City: Deseret Book Co., 1988], p. 23.)

Thus the Savior was not demanding perfect lives— no sin, no mistakes, no weaknesses or inadequacies. What he was admonishing us to do was to *become* perfect or exalted by partaking of his atonement and the rest of the plan of salvation through faith, repentance, obedience, and faithful endurance. Drawing upon our spiritual resources we are to make every effort to overcome our sins and weaknesses in this life as we steadily reach toward perfection. But even after "all we can do" we only become "complete" or "finished" as we are resurrected and exalted through the tender mercies of Christ.

Of the process of perfection, President Joseph Fielding Smith testified:

> Salvation does not come all at once; we are commanded to be perfect even as our Father in heaven is perfect. It will take us ages to accomplish this end, for there will be greater progress beyond the grave, and it will be there that the faithful will overcome all things, and receive all things, even the fulness of the Father's glory.
>
> I believe the Lord meant just what he said: that we should be perfect, as our Father in heaven is perfect. That will not come all at once, but line upon line, and precept upon precept, example upon example, and even then not as long as we live in this mortal life, for we will have to go even beyond the grave before we reach that perfection and shall be like God. (*Doctrines of Salvation*, Bruce R. McConkie, comp., 3 vols. [Salt Lake City: Bookcraft, 1954–56], 2:18–19.)

An unrealistic expectation that we must be perfect in all we do in this life becomes an overwhelming burden that actually retards true gospel living and stifles spirituality. When we fall short of our preconceived notions of perfection (as we always will in this life), we tend to browbeat ourselves with undeserved self-criticism and guilt or to exhaust ourselves with unrealistic efforts to "work" our way to perfection. The more we stubbornly seek to perfect ourselves—solely by our own efforts and self-discipline—and knowingly or subconsciously refuse the merciful help of the Lord, we sink dangerously deeper into the quicksands of perfectionism. Just as the cowboy heroes of our past could only be rescued from quicksand through the assistance of another—be it human or horse—we too then need to stop flailing helplessly and rely on another whose strength alone can save us. Nephi taught that the only way we can *become* perfect is by "unshaken faith in [Christ], relying wholly upon the merits of him who is mighty to save," at the same time "[pressing] forward with a steadfastness in Christ" (2 Nephi 31:19–20). When we use and/or hear the phrase "perfect ourselves" we must not construe it to mean that we do it all on our own, but rather that we do our part—by doing the best we can—and the Savior will then do the rest.

While it is true that we can never "perfect ourselves," we *can* become "perfect in Christ." Moroni admonished:

> Yea, come unto Christ, and be perfected in him, and deny yourselves of all ungodliness; and if ye shall deny yourselves of all ungodliness, and love God with all your might, mind and strength, then is his grace sufficient for you, that by his grace ye may be perfect in Christ; and if by the grace of God ye are perfect in Christ, ye can in nowise deny the power of God.
>
> And again, if ye by the grace of God are perfect in Christ, and deny not his power, then are ye sanctified in Christ by the grace of God, through the shedding of the blood of Christ, which is in the covenant of the Father unto the remission of your sins, that ye become holy, without spot. (Moroni 10:32–33.)

Understanding the doctrine of perfection can liberate us from self-defeating behaviors and the destructive discouragement that destroy the faith in Christ that is necessary to allow him to make us perfect. When we come to know in our minds and understand in our hearts that Christ will lift us from the quicksand of perfectionism *if we allow him,* then our quest for perfection can become a joyful journey—for we know we are not alone. "God's demand for perfection need not discourage you in the least in your present attempts to be good, or even in your present failures," wrote the noted Christian author C. S. Lewis.

> Each time you fall He will pick you up again. And He knows perfectly well that your own efforts are never going to bring you anywhere near perfection. On the other hand, you must realise from the outset that the goal toward which He is beginning to guide you is absolute perfection; and no power in the whole universe, except you yourself, can prevent Him from taking you to that goal. . . .
>
> . . . The command Be ye perfect is not idealistic gas. Nor is it a command to do the impossible. He is going to make us into creatures that can obey that command. He said (in the Bible) that we were "gods" and He is going to make good His words. If we let Him—for we can prevent Him, if we choose—He will make the feeblest and filthiest of us into a god or goddess, dazzling, radiant, immortal creature, pulsating all through with such energy and joy and wisdom and love as we cannot now imagine, a bright stainless mirror which reflects back to God perfectly . . . His own boundless power and delight and goodness. The process will be long and in parts very painful; but that is what we are in for. Nothing less. He meant what He said. (*Mere Christianity* [New York: Macmillan, 1952], pp. 172, 174–75.)

Some people may fully understand the doctrinal teachings of perfection, recognize that we cannot be perfect in mortality, and acknowledge our ultimate dependence upon the Lord, yet fall prey to another aspect of perfectionism that can also destroy the spiritual balance of their lives. This dangerous attitude manifests itself not just in matters of sin and righteousness but also in our efforts to be the "perfect mother" or "perfect father" *and* the "perfect spouse" *and* the "perfect church worker" *and* the "perfect neighbor." The list could go on and on. So many of us have guilt feelings that we are not all that we should be because we cannot be all things to all people and perfect in all of those expectations—even though we exhaust ourselves physically and become drained emotionally in trying to do so. We sometimes find ourselves worrying that we didn't say the perfect thing, react in the perfect way, or do the perfect job at whatever we undertake. (This attitude is also like quicksand, because the harder we try to be what we want ourselves to be, and to do the "perfect job" at everything others expect of us, the more distraught we become because we can never quite measure up to our self-set standards of perfection.) Elder M. Russell Ballard, in speaking to the women of the Church, described this common dilemma that afflicts not only many women but also many men.

Some of you very likely are striving to be "supermoms." You feel a need to spend time with your husband and children. You want to be sure to have family prayer, read the scriptures, and have family home evening. You also feel the need to help children with homework and music lessons; keep your home presentable; prepare nutritious meals; keep clothes clean and mended; chauffeur children and possibly their friends to school and to a variety of lessons, practices, and games; and keep everyone in the family on schedule, making sure they are where they should be when they should be there. And that is all within your family and home. It makes me weary just reviewing all of this! It doesn't include PTA, volunteer service, or caring for family members who are ill or aged. You feel the need to protect your family from the many evil influences in the world such as suggestive television, films, and videos; alcohol; drugs; and pornography. You are committed to and faithfully fulfill your Church callings. In addition, many of you must earn a living because financial pressures are real and cannot be ignored. If anything is left or neglected, you feel that you have failed.

. . . I saw a bumper sticker the other day . . . that may say it all: "God put me on earth to accomplish a certain number of things. Right now I am so far behind, I will never die!" ("Be an Example of the Believers," *Ensign,* November 1991, p. 95.)

How can we better balance our lives spiritually, manage these overwhelming feelings of inadequacy, overcome emotional and spiritual burnout, and escape the quicksand of overexpectation before we drown? A better understanding of the scriptures and of the Lord's loving expectations of us will help liberate us from undeserved guilt and unnecessary discouragement. King Benjamin's counsel to not run faster than we have strength is as significant (if not more so) spiritually as it is temporally. The key phrase in his counsel that should guide us in our quest for spiritual balance is "be diligent." If we are diligent and approach the "spiritual demands" upon us with wisdom and order we will find abundance rather than anguish, delight rather than discouragement, and faith rather than frustration. We will discover that progress actually comes faster when we learn to do a few things well rather than many things by the skin of our teeth.

Further, we must remember that much spiritual growth occurs not suddenly but only through time and experience. The encouraging message of the gospel is that God does not often require sensational or extraordinary deeds of us but merely requires that we continually try to do a little better today than we did yesterday. He desires that we do things "in wisdom and in order"—steady progress, not spurts of spirituality; firmness of resolve, not flashy but fleeting results. He is mindful as much of our desires, our determination, and our direction as he is of our deeds. The Lord neither expects nor desires us to do more than we can—or more than that which is wise, but he desires that we diligently and steadily keep moving in the right direction.

Elder Ballard offered this wise counsel to help us maintain our spiritual and emotional bearings even when we feel that we can never measure up:

> To you who feel harried and overwhelmed and who wonder whether you ever will be able to run fast enough to catch the departing train you think you should be on, I suggest that you learn to deal with each day as it comes, doing the best you can, without feelings of guilt or inadequacy. . . .
>
> . . . Recognize limitations; no one can do everything. When you have done the best you can, be satisfied and don't look back and second-guess, wondering how you could have done more. Be at peace within yourselves. Rather than berate yourself for what you didn't do, congratulate yourself for what you did. ("Be an Example of the Believers," p. 95.)

The author John Steinbeck wrote of one of his characters in the novel *East of Eden*, "Now that she knew she didn't have to be perfect, she could be good." Being good and doing the best we can—whatever that may be—is doing the "all we can do" (2 Nephi 25:23) that will lead to our salvation and ultimate perfection. President Brigham Young declared:

> Those who do right, and seek the glory of the Father in heaven, . . . whether they can do little or much, if they do the very best they know how, they are perfect. . . . To be as perfect as we possibly can according to our knowledge, is to be just as perfect as our Father in Heaven is. . . . When we are doing as well as we know in the sphere, and station which we occupy here we are justified. . . . We are as justified as the angels who are before the throne of God. (*Deseret News Weekly,* 31 August 1854, p. 1, as quoted in *Melchizedek Priesthood Personal Study Guide 1,* 1988, p. 144.)

Even as we strive to "be diligent," as King Benjamin counselled, and to "do right, and seek the glory of the Father," as Brigham Young advised, sometimes we may still feel overwhelmed and inadequate. To maintain spiritual balance we must frequently take inventory of our spiritual progress. Honest assessment of the desires of our hearts and the direction of our lives will aid us in overcoming "these vexing feelings of inadequacy." Elder Neal A. Maxwell has provided us with these insightful suggestions that are both helpful and hopeful:

> We can distinguish more clearly between divine discontent and the devil's dissonance, between dissatisfaction with self and disdain for self. We need the first and must shun the second, for when conscience calls to us from the next ridge, it is not solely to scold but also to beckon.
>
> We can contemplate how far we have already come in the climb along the pathway to perfection; it is usually much further than we acknowledge, and such reflections restore resolve. . . .

We can make quiet but more honest inventories of our strengths. Most of us are dishonest bookkeepers and need confirming "outside auditors." He who in the first estate was thrust down delights in having us put ourselves down. Self-contempt is of Satan; there is none of it in heaven. We should, of course, learn from our mistakes, but without forever viewing the instant replays lest these become the game of life itself. . . .

We can know that when we have *truly* given what we have, it is like paying a full tithe; it is, in that respect, *all* that was asked. . . .

Finally we can accept this stunning, irrevocable truth: Our Lord can lift us from deep despair and cradle us midst any care. . . .

This is a gospel of grand expectations, but God's grace is sufficient for each of us if we remember that there are no *instant* Christians. (*Notwithstanding My Weakness*, pp. 9–11.)

Finally, and perhaps most important, we must remember, as Elder Maxwell has counselled, that we have the gift and aid of the grace of Christ in our lives. One of the barriers to spiritual balance is "pseudo-self-reliance." This creates an "I can handle it" attitude and a dangerous dependence upon our own efforts and works in seeking spiritual abundance.

As Wendy was attempting to drive herself to perfection and flagellating herself mercilessly for falling short, she discovered she was in a vicious cycle. She was experiencing what Robert L. Millet described as "a type of spiritual diminishing returns." "Some latter-day Saints, blocked in their [spiritual] progress . . . and . . . weighed down with guilt, seek to double their effort—to work harder. If the present pace does not eradicate the problem, they decide to run faster. Too often what follows is a type of spiritual diminishing returns—exhaustion and additional frustration. The answer to all problems is not necessarily more and harder work, particularly in . . . spiritual matters." (*Life in Christ* [Salt Lake City: Bookcraft, 1990], pp. 47–48.)

As mentioned, while Wendy was struggling to escape from this cycle of faithful works followed by the frustration and discouragement that characterize the quicksands of perfectionism, the Spirit whispered to her that what she was demanding of herself was not pleasing to the Lord because she was not allowing the atonement of Jesus Christ to have full operation in her life. It is not a sign of weakness to abandon pseudo-self-reliance and avail ourselves of the Atonement; rather it is a gesture of deep gratitude, love, and humility. The Atonement not only allows for repentance of sin but also permits us to forgive ourselves and receive the outpouring of his grace that strengthens and helps us when we simply do not have the power to overcome our human weaknesses on our own. A greater understanding of and faith in the power of the Atonement brings our lives into spiritual balance by allowing the Savior to share our burdens and compensate for our many inadequacies (see Matthew 11:28; Ether 12:27). As Robert L. Millet insightfully counselled:

In a day when the winds are blowing and the waves beating upon our ship, how do we navigate our course safely into the peaceful harbor? What must we do to have our Savior pilot us through tempestuous seas? Amidst the babble of voices—enticing voices which threaten to lead us into forbidden paths or which beckon us to labor in secondary causes—how do the Saints of the Most High know the Way, live the Truth, and gain that Life which is abundant? . . .

. . . We must learn to trust in him more, in the arm of flesh less. We must learn to rely on him more, and on man-made solutions less. We must learn to surrender our burdens to him more. We must learn and work to our limits and then be willing to seek that grace or enabling power which will make up the difference, that sacred power which indeed makes all the difference! (*Life in Christ,* p. 108.)

There is no inward stillness for those whose lives are out of balance, either temporally or spiritually. Instead of their enjoying peace, their lives and emotions become tossed to and fro by the winds of discouragement and the storms of frustration. Just as the Savior stilled the storms on the Sea of Galilee (see Matthew 8:23–26), he will bless our lives with his calming, comforting influence if we will "press forward with a steadfastness in Christ" (2 Nephi 31:20) and allow him to lovingly lift us out of the quicksands of perfectionism. May we strive to maintain spiritual balance in our lives so that instead of laying waste our powers we will find the abundant life Jesus promised, find joy in living the gospel, and be strengthened and renewed so that we can render more meaningful service to God and to our fellowmen.

Chapter Four

"The Lord Looketh upon the Heart"

A Pattern for Righteous Judging

*T*he judgments we form about others and about ourselves have a permeating effect not only on our personal stability but also on the fabric of our Mormon culture itself. Making unrighteous and unmerciful judgments, we may make living the gospel more difficult and less rewarding than it should be by creating a standard that no one can measure up to. On the other hand, if we can learn to judge one another—including ourselves—righteously we can build and nourish each other in the way that would be expected of true disciples of Christ. "By this shall all men know that ye are my disciples, if ye have love one to another" (John 13:35).

Righteous Judgment of Others

While strolling through a mall with her uncle, our seven-year-old daughter made an unabashed observation about a rather skimpy dress on a woman shopper. The uncle later reported to us that she had proclaimed to him, "That dress isn't very modest!" Rather than being offended at her frankness, he made the comment that he was impressed that she had passed judgment on the dress and not on the woman. He probably thought we had taught her that and we were happy to let him think it.

Actually, we breathed a sigh of relief, because our young children, like most, saw the world in very simple terms. We found that when we would teach them that smoking, for instance, was wrong and bad for us, they would automatically assume that anyone who smoked was bad. This posed a dilemma, because some of our favorite relatives smoked. As we taught from the Book of Mormon about the righteous Nephites and the wicked Lamanites, one of the children asked if some Lamanite members of our ward were wicked. We were also chagrined one day when one of our daughters asked a relative who was not active in the Church if she was a Mormon. The relative replied without hesitation that she was. Our daughter, being well drilled in the Word of Wisdom, proceeded to interrogate, "Then why do you drink coffee?" We began to realize that we would have to go to great lengths to teach our children to judge actions without judging the actor and to look past the outward appearances and distractions into the depths of the heart.

As we were teaching our children this lesson, we were learning it ourselves. We became aware of our own quickness to judge others and even ourselves by appearances and by meaningless and sometimes un-merciful standards. We noticed that we and many others in the Church were assessing ourselves, our fellow members, and our fellowmen with the simplistic, "black and white" understanding of a child.

"Judge not, that ye be not judged" from Christ's Sermon on the Mount is probably one of the most oft-quoted adages in the Bible. Even people who have never opened a Bible seem to be acquainted with it. Its intent is noble, but in practice we must make all kinds of judgments, or at least appraisals, every day, even about other people. One of the reasons why we were sent here was to learn to make wise judgments. We base the decisions we make every day on the judgments we have formed. It helps that the Prophet Joseph Smith was inspired to retranslate the passage into these words: "Judge not unrighteously, that ye be not judged: but judge righteous judgment" (JST Matthew 7:1–2).

While only God the Father and his Son, Jesus Christ, have the right to pass ultimate judgment on any soul, to the extent that we must also judge our fellowman we must emulate these two beings as nearly as possible. Judging as God would judge is "righteous judgment." Men tend to judge by many peripheral criteria, but the scriptures tell us that "the Lord seeth not as man seeth; for man looketh on the outward appearance, but the Lord looketh on the heart" (1 Samuel 16:7).

Because of our limited mortal perception it is true that sometimes we must judge initially by outward appearance and actions. We must judge whether a person's bearing and behavior is something we want to emulate or to avoid. In some circumstances we may have to evaluate whether, to what extent, and in what way we want to associate with the people we meet each day. It would be a foolish use of judgment to form constant associations with those who would make us less than we are, simply because we don't want to appear "judgmental." On the other hand, it would be a haughty and unmerciful use of judgment to refuse any association with others, especially loved ones, based only on outward demeanor.

We must remember, however, that judging the outward man, ourselves as well as others, is only the beginning of judgment. We must then temper that assessment with a Christlike love and compassion, remembering that, as one of our favorite LDS hymns says, "In the quiet heart is hidden sorrow that the eye can't see" ("Lord, I Would Follow Thee," *Hymns,* no. 220). There are endless instances of this in every life. A Primary president told of one of her teachers who harshly condemned the secretary of the Primary for asking to be released from her calling. This stalwart and uncompromising woman considered it a lack of faithfulness on the secretary's part. However, she was not privy to one small bit of information the president knew but could not divulge—the secretary's marriage was on the verge of collapse and she needed to spend more time with her husband and family.

We seldom know all the circumstances surrounding a person's life and the way he or she has chosen or is forced to live it. Perhaps the intents of the heart are much nobler than the behavior, which may be hampered by a lack of knowledge or understanding or by weaknesses yet to be overcome. It might be that the person has actually made a great deal of progress and is doing the best he or she can. Or it may simply be a matter of the differences in spiritual progression among spirits. Each one of God's children has the agency-endowed right to walk his own path, even if it zigzags wildly sometimes or proceeds with almost imperceptible progress. Elder H. Burke Peterson once cautioned, "If you are prone to criticize or judge, remember, we never see the target a man aims at in life. We see only what he hits." ("Removing the Poison of an Unforgiving Spirit," *Ensign,* November 1983, p. 60.) In other words, we must give a person every benefit of the doubt, not to excuse what he does but to try to understand it. We must endeavor as best we can to "look upon the heart" in judging others.

Elder Dallin H. Oaks demonstrated the importance of this principle in referring to the labels we give each other as members of the Church.

> We tend to think of members in categories according to "activity": active, less active, inactive, and so on. These categories are defined according to observable actions, notably attendance at Church meetings. They take little or no account (positive or negative) of the things of the heart. This is a misleading omission.
>
> A person may love God with all his or her heart, might, mind, and strength, and still be in a circumstance in which it is impossible or extremely difficult to do the actions that are customarily judged to constitute "activity." . . .
>
> Even where a person is "less active" because of carelessness or indifference, it is well to remember that the contrast between this member and some apparently active members may be quite different than meets the eye. Consider the contrast between deficiencies in actions and deficiencies in motives and attitudes. Who is more acceptable to God, a man who is indifferent to God and his fellowmen but attends church regularly to promote his business interests, or a man who loves God and his fellowmen but rarely attends meetings? Both of

these men are missing blessings and growth. Both have need to change. But which is in a better position to bring himself into total harmony with God? Attendance patterns can be altered in an instant. A new resolve, proven by subsequent conduct, can repair inaction. But a defect of the heart is much more serious and requires far more time and effort to repair. (*Pure in Heart* [Salt Lake City: Bookcraft, 1988], pp. 31–32.)

Furthermore, we may find that, given the same set of circumstances, we would also make the same or even less desirable choices than the person we are judging. It is very easy to criticize others who are weak in an area in which we have never been tempted or tested beyond our comfort zone. A man who considered himself very strong and self-sufficient criticized his daughter for taking tranquilizers to help her through a very difficult time. "You'd never see me taking tranquilizers!" he boasted contemptuously, wounding her already discouraged sensitivities. Not too many years later he suffered a failure in business and became so distraught that his doctor prescribed tranquilizers, which he gratefully accepted. Humbled by her own trials, his daughter never pointed this out to him, but did what she could to help him. It is ironic that believing we are impervious to someone else's sin or problem is often the first step toward committing or experiencing it ourselves—"Pride goeth before a fall," as the old Puritan saying goes. Lloyd Shearer penned this incisive admonition— "Resolve to be tender with the young, compassionate with the aged, sympathetic with the striving, and tolerant of the weak and the wrong. Sometime in life you will have been all of these."

This is one of the greatest lessons we can learn in

this life. It boils down to the principle of reciprocity, which is taught over and over again in the Savior's earthly sermons. You will receive what you are willing to give. Just as we can only be forgiven if we forgive (see Matthew 6:14–15), we will only be judged mercifully if we judge with mercy. Christ warned, "For with what judgment ye judge, ye shall be judged: and with what measure ye mete, it shall be measured to you again" (Matthew 7:2). The prophet Moroni reiterated this concept even more strongly: "For behold, the same that judgeth rashly shall be judged rashly again; for according to his works shall his wages be" (Mormon 8:19). This doesn't necessarily mean that others will be intolerant if we are intolerant (though this may be one side effect) but that *God* will not be able to extend *his* grace to us in *his* judgment of us, which obviously is the assessment that counts. In other words, he may have to judge us by our puny actions only and not on the intents of our heart. He may have to demand perfection of us because we demanded it of others. Perhaps he will be forced to withhold his understanding and compassion from us because we withheld it from others. In such a case, judgment day would be a "great and dreadful day" indeed (D&C 2:1), for no matter how flawless our works, they alone have no power to save us. Without the Lord's grace and mercy we are lost.

Once we have judged the behavior as compassionately as possible we must still distinguish between the sin and the sinner. The story of Christ and the woman taken in adultery is the perfect pattern.

> And the scribes and Pharisees brought unto him a woman taken in adultery; and when they had set her in the midst,

They say unto him, Master, this woman was taken in adultery, in the very act.

Now Moses in the law commanded us, that such should be stoned: but what sayest thou?

This they said, tempting him, that they might have to accuse him. But Jesus stooped down, and with his finger wrote on the ground, as though he heard them not.

So when they continued asking him, he lifted up himself, and said unto them, He that is without sin among you, let him first cast a stone at her.

And again he stooped down, and wrote on the ground.

And they which heard it, being convicted by their own conscience, went out one by one, beginning at the eldest, even unto the last: and Jesus was left alone, and the woman standing in the midst.

When Jesus had lifted up himself, and saw none but the woman, he said unto her, Woman, where are those thine accusers? hath no man condemned thee?

She said, No man, Lord. And Jesus said unto her, Neither do I condemn thee: go, and sin no more. (John 8:3–11.)

The first lesson we learn from this incident in the Savior's life is to remember our own sins and weaknesses when judging others and to admit, as suggested previously, that perhaps if we were in a similar situation we might have done no better. Furthermore, our sins are more serious to us than the sins of another because they are *our* sins, the ones we should be most concerned about. Another aspect we must consider is whether our harsh judgment of another is in itself a more serious problem than whatever we are condemning. One of our hymns cautions: "Should you feel inclined to censure faults you may in others view, ask your own heart, ere you venture, if you have not failings, too" (*Hymns,* no. 235). All of these considerations reflect the principle of the beam and the mote, also expounded by the Savior in the Sermon on the Mount. "And why beholdest thou the mote that is in thy brother's eye, but considerest not the beam that is in thine own eye? Or how wilt thou say to thy brother, Let me pull out the mote out of thine eye; and, behold, a beam is in thine own eye? Thou hypocrite, first cast out the beam out of thine own eye; and then shalt thou see clearly to cast out the mote out of thy brother's eye." (Matthew 7:3–5.)

Even worse, we might also have sins which are just as bad as or far more egregious than another person's but which are deceptively hidden from the judging eyes of others. Jesus saved his most condemnatory pronouncements for the hypocritical scribes and Pharisees: "Now do ye Pharisees make clean the outside of the cup and the platter; but your inward part is full of ravening and wickedness" (Luke 11:39). Judging by outward appearances these rulers would have been models of piety, but the Lord "looketh upon the heart." Thus, before we can justly condemn the actions of others, we should humbly examine our own souls and confess our own sins.

In contrast to the hypocritical scribes and Pharisees, in this story we have a woman who not only could not hide her sin but also was taken in the very act. Certainly that act was worthy of condemnation. But the Savior had only love, mercy, and compassion for her. By no means did he condone the sin. He made it clear that she should discontinue her wicked ways, but he gave her another chance. Undoubtedly she would be more motivated to repent by his divine love and compassionate acceptance of her despite her sin than she would have been by a harsh judgmental rebuke that would have filled her with fear and self-loathing. Thus it is whenever we must judge the actions of our fellowman and our own behavior as well. Love is always a more profound motivator than condemnation.

This principle of changing one's behavior because of the influence of divine love as opposed to divine wrath seems to be borne out in the literature on near-death experiences. While these experiences are not scripture or doctrine, they bear the mark of truth. Those who had "passed" to the other side almost always reported a meeting with a "being of light" who waited with them as they viewed a sort of replay of their lives (not the final judgment). Both the good and bad—everything they had ever done, and every thought they had ever had—were on display before them. Yet not one felt any disapproval or condemnation from the "being of light" (who may have represented Christ). They felt only complete, consuming love and acceptance in his presence, not for their sins but for their souls. While this being helped them learn from their mistakes, the most negative judgment passed upon them was that which they passed on themselves. When they returned to mortality, their overwhelming desire and determination to be better people came not from fear of judgment but from a longing to please and be with that "being of light"; to feel that infinite love once more. (See Brent L. Top and Wendy C. Top, *Beyond Death's Door* [Salt Lake City: Bookcraft, 1993], pp. 83–118.)

To judge "righteous judgment," then, is to judge with love—the pure love of Christ. This is a gift not obtained merely by wishing for it. Mormon tells us to "pray unto the Father with all the energy of heart, that ye may be filled with this love." Wherein we must judge others we must also pray, as Solomon did, for an "understanding heart to judge thy people" (1 Kings 3:9). In answer to Solomon's prayer, "God gave Solomon wisdom and understanding exceeding much, and largeness of heart, even as the sand that is on the sea shore" (1 Kings 4:29). Given such understanding we may sift through all the outward distractions and superficial measurements and attempt to look into the heart, not only in judging others but also in judging ourselves.

Righteous Self-Judgment

The principle of not judging others unrighteously, then, can also apply to our treatment or judgment of ourselves. Usually we would never be as unreasonably harsh or condemning of others as we often are of ourselves, and yet the love of Christ is just as much available to us as to anyone else. Elder Neal A. Maxwell cautioned, as quoted in chapter 3: "He who in the first estate was thrust down delights in having us put ourselves down. Self-contempt is of Satan; there is none of it in heaven." (*Notwithstanding My Weakness*, p. 10.)

On a television program, a teenage girl was struggling with her own awkward looks in comparison to her mother and to some of the popular girls at her high school. She thought they had everything they needed to be happy and accepted by others, but she came to find out that they too were hard on themselves and unable to enjoy their own beauty. At the end of the program she concluded something like this: "We are all in prison, and the crime is how much we hate ourselves." This is a distressing but profoundly true comment. We not only damn our own progress by unrighteously judging others but also, more seriously, by brutally condemning ourselves. If we allowed ourselves to feel as much of Christ's love as we would want others to feel, we could set ourselves free from the chains of self-contempt that enslave us and smother our happiness and potential.

Our need to open ourselves to the pure love of Christ is central because this love is a far greater motivation to righteousness and repentance than the unrelenting and merciless self-reproach many of us often heap upon ourselves. We need to stifle our own castigating consciences and calmly listen for the gentle, merciful guidance of his Spirit. If we have truly done wrong, the Savior then will make it known by filling us with "godly sorrow" for our sins instead of the "sorrow of the world," which "worketh death" (see 2 Corinthians 7:9–10). Godly sorrow causes us to love God and desire to be reconciled to him and feel his approbation rather than discouraging and disheartening us and making us hate ourselves. Self-flagellation is not pleasing to the Lord. Perhaps, considering all he has given us, it is even insulting and ungrateful. Ironically, we may somehow feel that if we punish and downgrade ourselves enough we will finally be worthy of forgiveness for our inadequacies. Not so ironically, this only makes us feel more unworthy. Elder Richard G. Scott, speaking of forgiving ourselves for past mistakes and sins, illustrated a principle which perhaps might also apply to harshly and unjustly judging ourselves.

> If you, through poor judgment, were to cover your shoes with mud, would you leave them that way? Of course not. You would cleanse and restore them. Would you then gather the residue of mud and place it in an envelope to show others the mistake that you made? No. Neither should you continue to relive forgiven sin.

Every time such thoughts come into your mind, turn your heart in gratitude to the Savior, who gave His life that we, through faith in Him and obedience to His teachings, can overcome transgression and conquer its depressing influence in our lives. ("We Love You—Please Come Back," *Ensign,* May 1986, p. 12.)

A favorite story illustrates how we unnecessarily deprive ourselves of the joy we might have if we could only understand the love and mercy we are offered. A woman who mopped floors for a living had wanted all her life to take a cruise on an ocean liner. For years she deprived herself and scraped, scrimped, and saved every penny she could until she finally had enough money for the fare. Since it would simply take her too long to save the money to pay for her meals also, she brought enough cheese and crackers on the trip to last the entire time. Every mealtime, when others were feasting on the sumptuous food in the dining hall, she would quietly nibble her cheese and crackers in some sunny corner of the deck.

On the last day of the cruise, the captain happened to walk by and ask her why she was only eating cheese and crackers for her meal. When she replied that she couldn't afford to eat the fancy fare available in the dining room, he exclaimed, "But the cost of your meals was included in the price of your ticket!"

As a child of God, each of us is offered the same love that he shows to others. It is part of the package, yet often we find it easier to see how it applies to others than how it applies to ourselves. Thus we withhold from ourselves the full banquet of life, thinking we can't permit ourselves such a luxury.

Moreover, one of the most delicious and fulfilling experiences of life is learning to feel the pure love of Christ in one's own life. One way to do this is by judging ourselves righteously. As Elder Maxwell observed, "We can make quiet but more honest inventories of our strengths" (*Notwithstanding My Weakness*, p. 10). As we seek diligently to work out our salvation, we must be fair with ourselves at times when we falter. Instead of torturing ourselves, we can speak gently, though truthfully, to ourselves as we would to a troubled friend or our own erring child; we can help, encourage, and understand ourselves as we would a lonely stranger in need; we can be patient and supportive, though firm, with ourselves as we would with family members or other loved ones in crisis. In other words, we must learn to treat ourselves as Jesus Christ would have us treat ourselves. Only then can we see ourselves as he sees us and become what he would have us be.

In conclusion, being unfairly critical and unrighteously judgmental of ourselves and others affects our spiritual and emotional well-being not only as individuals but also as a community of Saints. Comparing ourselves to others or others to ourselves is a lose/lose proposition for all of us. It creates competition rather than cooperation, promotes show over substance, and fosters a disregard for our divine individuality. Personally, it disrupts our private peace and, if unchecked, becomes a vicious cycle which destroys the "inward stillness" that comes only from the approving witness of the Holy Spirit. The Lord has taught his Saints that all final condemnation is his alone. "For all flesh is in mine hands; be still and know that I am God" (D&C 101:16).

Chapter Five

Overcoming Fear

Through Faith, Hope, and Charity

*I*n our lives, we (Wendy and Brent) have also found fear to be a paramount obstacle to living the gospel in the steady, serene, and sincere way it is meant to be lived. Fears ranging from fear of failure and fear of what others may think to fear of losing loved ones and fear of one's own death can prevent one from internalizing and really understanding the profound peace that only the true gospel of Jesus Christ can create within us. Yet this powerful peace is our only real protection against the very fear we fear. Thus, winning the battle against fear breaks this paralyzing cycle and empowers us to withstand one of Satan's most effective and destructive tools in these last days.

The Prophet Joseph Smith described section 88 in the Doctrine and Covenants as "the olive leaf which we have plucked from the Tree of Paradise, the Lord's message of peace to us" (*History of the Church* 1:316). Despite the symbolism of the olive leaf as a "message of peace," the Lord warns in that same section that in the last days "all things shall be in commotion; and surely, men's hearts shall fail them; for fear shall come upon all people" (v. 91). For years Wendy thought that heart attacks were a sign of the Second Coming! Yet when *her* heart threatened to fail her because of fear, she began to understand the real meaning of the scripture. It wasn't a "coronary occlusion" she suffered but a loss and a lack of "heart"—faith, courage, will to go on. As the old song advises, "You gotta have heart."

As a young mother with three babies to watch over, she was nearly overcome with fear. Being responsible for three delicate lives suddenly made her acutely aware of all the evil and unfortunate possibilities in the world. She thought this fearfulness was an inescapable burden of motherhood, until it made her so miserable that she began to be physically sick and unable to fully function in her daily responsibilities. At that point she realized that something was seriously wrong in her life. The scriptural phrase "men are, that they might have joy" (2 Nephi 2:25) kept running through her mind. It occurred to her then that perhaps fear did not have to be a constant fact of life. She wondered if the Lord intended fear to fill any helpful role in our lives.

In searching the scriptures she found answers to her questions and strength and guidance to overcome her weakness. The Lord has a great deal to say to his children on the subject of fear. This overpowering emotion has been a potential stumbling block to men and women since Adam and Eve (see LDS Bible Dictionary, p. 672, hereafter cited as BD). As she pondered the passages she had discovered, she felt that there were five basic messages in the scriptures about fear.

First, *the only healthy fear is a fear of God.* This fear of God is not a negative emotion. The LDS Bible Dictionary explains that this kind of fear "is equivalent to reverence, awe, worship, and is therefore an essential part of the attitude of mind in which we ought to stand toward the All-holy God" (BD, p. 672). It has also been described simply as "caring what God thinks of you." This version of fear has to do with being respectful, humble, and obedient, not with being frightened. It is a fear that blesses us. "The fear of the Lord is the beginning of wisdom" (Psalm 111:10; see also Proverbs 15:16; Luke 1:50). Indeed, it is a fear we are commanded to possess. Ecclesiastes, or the Preacher, summarized: "Let us hear the conclusion of the whole matter: Fear God, and keep his commandments: for this is the whole duty of man" (Ecclesiastes 12:13; see also Proverbs 3:7; D&C 10:56).

Second, *"You should not . . . [fear] man more than God" (D&C 3:7).* Possessing the fear of God helps us conquer our fear of man. Knowing that ultimately it is God who will prevail and not man, we can say with the Psalmist, "In God I have put my trust; I will not fear what flesh can do unto me" (Psalm 56:4). There are frightening, even terrifying events around us in these last days. With the help of modern media we are reminded of them continually. We may even have to endure some of them, but we know this is all part of the test we agreed to in our premortal home. "Fear none of those things which thou shalt suffer: . . . be thou faithful unto death, and I will give thee a crown of life" (Revelation 2:10). Moreover, we should be more apprehensive about sin than we are about any of the terrors of the temporal world. Sin (over which we have a great deal of control) is the one thing that can keep us from our source of comfort and peace and from our final triumph over fear. The Savior cautioned in his day, "Fear not them which kill the body, but are not able to kill the soul: but rather fear him which is able to destroy both soul and body in hell" (Matthew 10:28).

The third message Wendy found was that *the Lord does intend that the wicked be fearful*—if not as a final means of bringing them to repentance, then as a natural consequence for their rebellion against the Almighty God. "But it is they who do not fear me, neither keep my commandments . . . that I will disturb, and cause to tremble and shake to the center" (D&C 10:56). The scriptures include ominous descriptions of the inescapable fear and awful dread which has and will come upon the wicked and unrepentant at a time of reckoning. Mormon hauntingly recorded that the intransigent Nephite people beheld the Lamanite army marching toward them "with that awful fear of death which fills the breasts of all the wicked" (Mormon 6:7). Isaiah, the poetic prophet, continually forewarned evil doers of the terror which would engulf them at the last day if they did not repent: "Fear, and the pit, and the snare, are upon thee, O inhabitant of the earth. And it shall come to pass, that he who fleeth from the noise of the fear shall fall into the pit; and he that cometh up out of the midst of the pit shall be taken in the snare: for the windows from on high are open, and the foundations of the earth do shake." (Isaiah 24:17–18.) Indeed, one of the most prevalent messages of the Old Testament prophets could be summarized as "fear to the wicked, peace to the righteous."

Correspondingly, the fourth message is that *the righteous need not fear.* This reassurance is often repeated in scripture. Isaiah's gentle descriptions of a promised peace were as soothing to the righteous as his forebodings of fear were frightful to the wicked. "And the work of righteousness shall be peace; and the effect of righteousness quietness and assurance for ever" (Isaiah 32:17). Furthermore, it seems that the righteous are being *commanded* not to fear. "Fear not" is a common admonition in holy writ. "Strip yourselves [of] . . . fears," the Lord told the early elders of the Church (D&C 67:10). Earlier still, when he walked upon the earth, the Savior exhorted his disciples, "Let not your heart be troubled, neither let it be afraid" (John 14:27). Finally, those who are faithful and careful and have tried to follow the counsel of the prophets can claim a special security in the often-quoted scripture which seems to be both a reassurance and a commandment: "If ye are prepared ye shall not fear" (D&C 38:30).

The fifth aspect of fear discussed in the scriptures often follows a commandment not to fear and is the most comforting and helpful. It is the strengthening and sustaining assurance that *we are not left alone to overcome our fears.* Again from Isaiah: "Fear thou not; for I am with thee: be not dismayed; for I am thy God: I will strengthen thee; yea, I will help thee; yea, I will uphold thee with the right hand of my righteousness" (Isaiah 41:10–13; see also Isaiah 35:4). The Savior continually encouraged Joseph Smith and the other members of the fledgling church not to be fearful of the overwhelming obstacles they faced. "Verily I say unto you my friends, fear not, let your hearts be comforted; yea, rejoice evermore" (D&C 98:1). "Wherefore, be of good cheer, and do not fear, for I the Lord am with you, and will stand by you" (D&C 68:6). Indeed, when we begin to trust in these unfailing promises of strength and succor from the Lord we will finally understand that, while we must always be faithful and careful, we *never* need to be fearful. "The Lord is my light and my salvation; whom shall I fear? the Lord is the strength of my life; of whom shall I be afraid?" (Psalm 27:1.)

Thus Wendy learned from the scriptures that fear was not of God. When the Apostle Paul was exhorting Timothy to go forth and use the gifts and talents the Lord had given him to spread the gospel, he counselled, "For God hath not given us the spirit of fear; but of power, and of love, and of a sound mind" (2 Timothy 1:7). In fact, she came to the conclusion that fear is one of the prime paralyzing ploys of Satan. Elder Derek H. Cuthbert of the Seventy spoke of the futility of fear. "It stifles initiative, saps strength, and reduces efficiency," he said. "It weakens faith, brings doubts, and begets mistrust. Indeed, it tends to impede the very business of being. How negative, frustrating, and futile is fear." ("The Futility of Fear," *Brigham Young University 1983–84 Fireside and Devotional Speeches* [Provo: University Publications, 1984], p. 105.) A friend of ours who has a counseling practice and helps others overcome personal obstacles is convinced that one of the greatest battles facing the "Saturday's Warriors" of today is the fight against fear. We will have to conquer our own fears before we can conquer evil and do good. As President Franklin D.

Roosevelt warned during the Great Depression, "The only thing we have to fear is fear itself."

Once Wendy understood that fear didn't have to be a part of her life, she realized also that this is easier said than done. However, the scriptures did not leave her without guidance. Another pattern began to emerge from her study. She discovered that the key to vanquishing her fears rested in three familiar words: faith, hope, and charity.

Faith

It was sobering to Wendy to discover that faith and fear are opposites. She had thought her faith strong, but she then realized that she was letting her fear devour her faith. The opposing nature of faith and fear became clear to her as she read of Peter walking on the water. He and the other disciples were aboard a ship, tossed violently about in the late hours of a stormy, dark night. Jesus approached the ship walking on the very waters of the Sea of Galilee.

The disciples were frightened, but Christ assured them, "Be of good cheer; it is I; be not afraid." Heartened and having faith, Peter desired to walk upon the water himself. The Savior consented, and Peter was actually able to defy the forces of gravity, partaking of the very power of the Christ himself. "But when he saw the wind boisterous, he was *afraid;* and beginning to sink, he cried, saying, Lord, save me. And immediately Jesus stretched forth his hand, and caught him, and said unto him, O thou of *little faith,* wherefore didst thou doubt?" (See Matthew 14:24–31, emphasis added.) Peter doubted because his fear of earthly forces chased away his faith in divine powers.

On another dark night when the wind and the sea were blustery and brooding, the Savior himself was on the storm-tossed ship with the disciples, but he was sleeping soundly through it all. Terrified that they would be lost in the tempest, his disciples awakened him abruptly, saying (as many of us also do when filled with anxiety), "Master, carest thou not that we perish?" After quietly and calmly stilling the storm, he gently chided his disciples. "Why are ye so fearful? how is it that ye have no faith?" (See Mark 4:37–40.) Faith is the antidote for fear.

Just as faith is the cure for fear, fear can sicken and cripple faith and deprive us of its benefits and blessings. Again, the Lord taught his newly restored church: "Ye endeavored to believe that ye should receive the blessing which was offered unto you; but behold, verily I say unto you there were fears in your hearts, and verily this is the reason that ye did not receive" (D&C 67:3). Just as on the stages of our minds the battle can rage between virtuous and unworthy thoughts, so goes the battle in our hearts between faith and fear. We must fight fearfulness incessantly by praying and striving for the gift of faith continually. In his address on fear, Elder Cuthbert offered this noble declaration by Emily Brontë, among the last lines she wrote, which embodies the determination we all need to employ.

No coward soul is mine,
No trembler in the world's storm-troubled sphere:
I see Heaven's glories shine,
And faith shines equal, arming me from fear.

Hope

Hope and faith are so closely and completely linked that sometimes it may be impossible for human minds to discern a great deal of difference between them. Mormon tells us that we cannot have faith without hope nor hope without faith (see Moroni 7). Hope seems to add an even more uplifting dimension to faith. It is a profound and abiding optimism about life and the plan of salvation. The prophet Ether tells us that what we may hope for ultimately is eternal life through the atonement of Christ and for a better world hereafter (see Ether 12:4). Jesus Christ is the source of our hope as well as of our faith. Knowing that through him wholeness, righteousness, peace, and joy will one day triumph forever can help us endure a great deal faithfully. But we can also hope for a better world in this life as well. Rather than fearing a difficult future, we can hope and plan for a bright one. Since, as Mark Twain once said, most of the things we worry about never happen, we should infuse our hearts and minds with a hope for good things instead.

Children seem to possess naturally this "perfect brightness of hope" (2 Nephi 31:20). They remain untainted by the cynicism that often erodes our faith as we experience the ironies and disappointments of life. When our daughter Emma Jane was four years old, she became friends with a young woman next door who had been paralyzed in a car accident. Each night Emma Jane would kneel at her bedside to pray and unfailingly ask the Lord to "bless Kori that her legs will get better." One night Wendy tenderly tried to explain to Emma Jane that Kori would never walk again in this life. Emma Jane seemed undaunted. Her unequivocal reply was, "I know, but I can still hope." It was the most profound lesson on hope we have ever learned. She persisted in offering this simple petition for over two years, even after the young woman had moved away.

Emma Jane seemed to understand that even though things *might* not work out the way she wished, she could still at least keep trying and hoping. We don't have to pretend that the sun is shining when it isn't, but we must never give up hope that it will shine again. Meanwhile we can hope that blessings will come from trials and that everything that happens to us will be for our eternal advancement if we are faithful. Every cloud *does* have a silver lining. It isn't just a trite saying, but an eternal truth—if we are faithful. Finally, at the very least we always have the hope that comes from knowing that whatever fears we may have to face, the Lord will be with us, strengthen us, and do for us whatever we cannot do for ourselves. In this way he is truly "the hope of Israel, the saviour thereof in time of trouble" (Jeremiah 14:8).

Charity

Charity, or love, might seem at first to have little to do with conquering fear. However, the scriptures establish a definite connection. The Apostle John wrote, "There is no fear in love; but perfect love casteth out fear: because fear hath torment. He that feareth is not made perfect in love." (1 John 4:18.) Predicting dire consequences for those who perverted the ways of the Lord by advocating infant baptism, Mormon said, "I speak with boldness, having authority from God; and I fear not what man can do; for perfect love casteth out all fear" (Moroni 8:16). In a general conference address entitled "Be of Good Cheer," Elder Neal A. Maxwell attested that if we are fearful, it is because we do not love enough. "Alas, brothers and sisters, we likewise live in a time when the love of many will wax cold. (See D&C 45:27; Matthew 24:12.) Fear will therefore increase. Why?" Elder Maxwell then offered this important doctrinal explanation: "Because when men fear, it is because we are not perfect in love. The less love, the more fear—as well as the more war!" ("Be of Good Cheer," *Ensign,* November 1982, p. 67.)

Thus when we are filled with charity, the pure love of Christ, there is no room or need for fear in our hearts. The two cannot exist in the same place. Perhaps fear is somewhat born of selfishness—being worried and focused on ourselves and our problems. If we are filled with charity we are more concerned for others and have less time to be afraid for ourselves. Indeed, we often see how the urge to help others can overpower personal fears and give people courage and strength to perform deeds that once seemed dreadfully unimaginable. Moreover, if we love others as Christ would love them it is hard for us to be afraid of them. Our Savior epitomized the conquest of love over fear when he asked his Father to forgive those who nailed him to the cross.

Whether we are afraid that others will harm us physically or just feel insecure and intimidated in their presence, charity will eclipse our fears with compassion. Patricia Holland, wife of Elder Jeffrey R. Holland of the Quorum of the Twelve, spoke of the fruits of peace that come from conquering fear with love.

Dr. Gerald G. Jampolsky, a psychiatrist from the University of California, tells us that love is an innate characteristic. It's already there. But too often it becomes clouded over with fear, which, through life's experiences, we've conjured up ourselves. He says, "When you feel love for all, not just those you choose, but all those [with] whom you come in contact—you experience peace. When you feel fear with anyone you come in contact with, you want to defend yourselves and attack others and there comes the conflict." (Gerald Jampolsky, *Love Is Letting Go of Fear* [New York: Bantam Books, 1981], p. 2.). . . .

If the fear of other women and/or men causes our conflict, and unconditional love for them brings us the valued peace we so desire, then shouldn't the whole pursuit of our lives be to extend love everywhere and to everyone? Doesn't it make you want to put every ounce of energy you have into the practice and pursuit of perfect love? ("The Fruits of Peace," *Ensign,* June 1984, p. 50.)

Some fears become sicknesses for which we may need to seek practical, professional help just as we would go to a medical doctor for physical maladies. Nevertheless the principles of faith, hope, and charity still apply. In the years of relying on this formula for overcoming our fears, we (Wendy and Brent) have found it true without exception. It is effective against any kind of fear: realistic fears, fears of the unknown, phobias, fears of personal inadequacies, fears that hinder personal relationships, fears that cower deep in the heart and mind. Perhaps that is because faith, hope, and charity are the keys to all happiness. "Wherefore, there must be faith; and if there must be faith there must also be hope; and if there must be hope there must also be charity. And except ye have charity ye can in nowise be saved in the kingdom of God; neither can ye be saved in the kingdom of God if ye have not faith; neither can ye if ye have no hope. And if ye have no hope ye must needs be in despair." (Moroni 10:20–22.)

As with other spiritual qualities, there are many things we can do to foster faith, hope, and charity in our lives. We can pray, search the scriptures, sing hymns, give service, seek the Comforter, follow the living prophets, and measure up to our own individual capacity for righteousness. Above all, we must acknowledge that Jesus Christ is our consummate source of peace. We must turn to him not only for refuge but also to bless our souls with the very faith, hope, and charity we need to overcome our fears. We cannot create these qualities in ourselves. These three are gifts of grace which are bestowed upon us in a beneficent response to our own sincere efforts. We may supply the outward actions, but he supplies the essence. Mormon taught that we must "pray unto the Father with all the energy of heart, that ye may be filled with [charity], which he hath bestowed upon all who are true followers of his Son, Jesus Christ" (Moroni 7:48).

As we make our way through tremulous times in these last days, when "men's hearts are failing them for fear," we can learn from the lessons of Peter. While walking on the water, this disciple-in-training let his focus on Christ fade, if only momentarily, as he considered the seeming impossibility of his situation. We must not be distracted by the terrors of the world which surround us. We must not stop to consider or dwell on the things that *could* go wrong.

A former bishop and dear friend of ours piloted a cargo plane in and out of Vietnam during the war there, sometimes under intense fire. When we asked him how he kept from being overcome by fear in such harrowing situations, he explained that he was kept so busy just doing his job that he didn't have time to think or worry about it. We likewise must busy ourselves with doing our duty—with faith, hope, and charity. We must keep our "eyes on the prize"; our minds and our lives anchored on our only hope— Jesus Christ himself. As we do this, we will gain a sure testimony that the fears that are devouring the world on all sides of us will not affect us. We will live in a different reality. As Isaiah poetically promised, "Thou wilt keep him in perfect peace, whose mind is stayed on thee" (Isaiah 26:3).

Chapter Six

"That We May Do His Will, and Do That Only"

Living by the Spirit

*T*he simple key to finding the peace and balance we have discussed in this book is learning to live according to the promptings of the Holy Spirit. It is easy to identify but it takes a lifetime of constant labor to accomplish. It is the ultimate quest of our mortal lives.

> Let us then labor for an inward stillness,
> An inward stillness and an inward healing,
> That perfect silence where the lips and heart
> Are still, and we no longer entertain
> Our own imperfect thought and vain opinions,
> But God alone speaks in us, and we wait

In singleness of heart, that we may know
His will, and in the silence of our spirits,
That we may do His will, and do that only!

—Henry Wadsworth Longfellow

This is not a token daily consultation with God we are advocating, but a total, thorough, absolute submission to his will in all things at all times. We must overcome the human tendency to see all willful submission as some kind of weakness and loss of control and begin to see submission to God as the most courageous, enobling, and emancipated state we can attain. Brigham Young declared: "We cannot talk about spiritual things without connecting with them temporal things, neither can we talk about temporal things without connecting spiritual things with them. . . . We, as Latter-day Saints, really expect, look for and we will not be satisfied with anything short of being governed and controlled by the word of the Lord in all of our acts, both spiritual and temporal. If we do not live for this, we do not live to be one with Christ." (*Journal of Discourses* 10:329.) In his intercessory prayer, offered in the last private mortal moment with his Apostles, Christ prayed that those who believe in him might "all be one; as thou, Father, art in me, and I in thee, that they also may be one in us" (John 17:21). God the Father and his divine Son are one because of a perfect unity of will and purpose. To be one with them, we must submit to the will of God, even as our exemplar and Savior, a God himself, did (see Luke 22:42).

God does not require complete compliance and oneness with his will because he is a tyrannical taskmaster and receives sadistic pleasure in our subservience, but rather because he seeks lovingly to lift us up to his level—godhood. Godhood is a perfect power over all things, attained by a perfect submission to all righteousness and eternal truth. We can only acquire this power as we surrender ourselves to him and allow *him* to remake us. Even during a time of wickedness, persecution, and affliction, many Nephites discovered for themselves how this very literal process of perfection and becoming a god proceeds. "Nevertheless they did fast and pray oft, and did wax stronger and stronger in their humility, and firmer and firmer in the faith of Christ, unto the filling their souls with joy and consolation, yea, even to the purifying and the sanctification of their hearts, which sanctification cometh because of their yielding their hearts unto God" (Helaman 3:35). The prophet Nephi, the son of Helaman, further learned that submitting to the Lord's will engenders not helplessness and slavery but vast power and freedom:

> Blessed art thou, Nephi, for those things which thou hast done; for I have beheld how thou hast with unwearyingness declared the word, which I have given unto thee, unto this people. And thou hast not feared them, and hast not sought thine own life, but has sought my will, and to keep my commandments.
>
> And now, because thou hast done this with such unwearyingness, behold, I will bless thee forever; and I will make thee mighty in word and in deed, in faith and in works; yea, even that all things shall be done unto thee according to thy word, for thou shalt not ask that which is contrary to my will.
>
> Behold, thou art Nephi, and I am God. Behold, I declare it unto thee in the presence of mine angels, that ye shall have power over this people. (Helaman 10:4–6.)

So complete was the Lord's trust in Nephi and so perfectly was Nephi's will melded into the Lord's that Nephi was empowered to bring great calamity and destruction upon the Nephites and the Lamanites, if *he* chose, in order to bring about their repentance. This was indeed a godlike power granted to him. Likewise, as we become more willing that the Lord's will be done, he is more willing that our will also be done, because the two are becoming one and we have demonstrated that we would never desire that which is inharmonious with the promptings of the Holy Spirit. Thus we are granted the righteous desires of our hearts.

Not only should we seek the will of God for ourselves, but we should also continually encourage our families, fellow Saints, and other fellowmen to also look to the inner light. Life in these last days is becoming more confusing and perplexing and Satan is becoming more proficient in creating conditions in which the black and white guidelines of an easier time become blurred and sometimes humanly impossible to follow, no matter how upright the intents of our hearts. There may be dilemmas for which there are no preconceived solutions. We must support and strengthen each other to have the courage to follow the Spirit in spite of fear—whether it be fear of the opinions of others or fear of death. For those who "have taken the Holy Spirit for their guide, and have not been deceived . . . shall abide the [last] day[s]" (D&C 45:57).

How Do We Live by the Spirit?

Receiving revelation and guidance from God, as sensational as it may sound to some, is actually a very quiet, simple, and introspective way to live. Each person must come to know how the Spirit speaks to him or her, but as always the Lord has given some standards or basic examples for receiving inspiration.

We learn much from Oliver Cowdery's experience with trying to translate. As we know, he was unsuccessful, but he afterwards learned a great deal about the right way to receive revelation. He learned that he had to do his part first—study the problem or situation; come up with an idea or answer; and then ask the Lord if that was right (see D&C 9:6–9). Of course, we can even ask for guidance in this process, but the Lord wants us to learn to do some thinking on our own. He does not want spiritual robots. A remarkable amount of knowledge, understanding, and personal strength can come from this sifting, self-stretching process, especially when it concerns personal decisions.

This is the process we must repeat and refine in order to find out what it really is that the Lord requires of us in living his gospel. We have to come to know ourselves—our limitations, our capacities, our true desires, our real motives. We must search the scriptures diligently and intently so that we understand what the Lord, not society, expects of us. We then have to weigh those demands of gospel living against our own abilities and God-given missions in life, not against the expectations of others.

For instance, when someone gives a talk or makes a warning statement about some principle of the gospel we should be living better, we should ask ourselves, "How does the Lord want me to practice this principle in *my* life?" Of course, some commandments apply in the same way to everyone. "Thou shalt not commit adultery"—there is no wiggle room in that. But there are other directives that are more open-ended—like

"Love and serve one another." There are times in our lives when perhaps all we can do to implement this is to pray for others, even though no one but Heavenly Father may know. We may feel that this is inadequate because it doesn't *show* that we are trying to help, but it may actually be the most effective service of all. There will be other times and circumstances when we are capable of doing a great deal and the Lord will expect it of us. Further, since we can't do everything at once, just how and when we fit some principles or activities into our lives will have to be subject to the Lord's direction.

Following are excerpts from an article on temple and family history work in which Elder Dallin H. Oaks gives us excellent guidelines for proceeding with that important work. We could all profitably seek guidance as to how these can be applied to the responsibilities placed on us by the gospel in home, church, and community.

All members should participate by prayerfully selecting those ways that fit their personal circumstances at a particular time. This should be done under the influence of the Spirit of the Lord and with the guidance of priesthood leaders who issue calls and direct the Church-administered portions of this work. Our effort is not to compel everyone to do everything, but to encourage everyone to do something. . . .

Some members may feel guilty about not furthering the mission of the Church when they are actually doing so. This kind of guilt comes not from insufficient efforts, but from insufficient vision. For example, a mother with several young children may be furthering the mission of the Church most profoundly in all three of its dimensions [proclaim the gospel, perfect the Saints, redeem the dead] in her own home when she helps her children to prepare for missions, and when she teaches them to revere the temple and prepare to make covenants there, and when she shows them how to strive for perfection in their personal lives. . . .

Quotas or per capita assignments violate an important principle. In the past, most of us have heard a person give an assignment for every member of a quorum or Relief Society to attend the temple a certain number of times per month. In the past, most of us have observed a local leader make assessments for each member of a ward to contribute exactly the same amount of money for a particular financial need. Such assignments or assessments take no account of individual circumstances or the spirit of voluntary offering. Head-tax assessments require some to do more than they are able, and they require others to do less than they should. Assessments deny everyone the blessing of making a voluntary offering. . . .

In summary, we should understand and apply these principles:

(1) All things should be done in wisdom and order. We should recognize that our members have many individual circumstances. Considering these, we should promote the mission of the Church in such a way as to accomplish the work of the Lord, not to impose guilt on his children.

(2) There is a time to every purpose under the heaven. There are many tasks to be performed in temple and family history work. We should encourage our members to make a prayerful selection of the things they can do in their individual circumstances . . . being "diligent unto the end."

(3) Each member should think about the three dimensions of the mission of the Church—proclaiming the gospel, perfecting the Saints, redeeming the dead—as a lifelong personal assignment and privilege. Each should gauge his or her personal participation from time to time according to his or her own circumstances

and resources, as guided by the Spirit of the Lord and the direction of priesthood leaders. ("Family History: 'In Wisdom and Order,'" *Ensign,* June 1989, pp. 6–8.)

However, while living by the Spirit is more liberating than living by the letter of the law, it also requires greater accountability. If we choose to defer or eliminate something, we must be sure that decision is approved by the Lord. "Therefore to him that knoweth [by the Holy Ghost] to do good, and doeth it not, to him it is sin" taught James the Apostle (James 4:17). In fine, we must come to know our own personal best and have the courage to do it; and if the Lord affirms that he wants us to do something beyond our present abilities, he will provide a way for us to do it (see 1 Nephi 3:7).

Manifestations of Spirituality in Our Lives

From Oliver Cowdery's experience we learn that after we have studied the problem, arrived at an answer we feel good about, and asked the Lord if it is right, the Lord will confirm or deny our conclusion in keeping with some basic guidelines. According to his eternal pattern, we can always count on at least two witnesses—"in the mouth of two or three witnesses shall every word be established" (D&C 6:28). In the case of personal revelation, we perhaps may think of these two witnesses as being the mind and the heart. "Yea, behold, I will tell you in your mind and in your heart, by the Holy Ghost, which shall come upon you and which shall dwell in your heart" (D&C 8:2). The Lord told Oliver Cowdery that if what he had in his mind and had presented to the Lord was right, he would "cause that your bosom shall burn within you," the heart thereby bearing witness to what was in the head. The burning of the bosom is not everyone's way of receiving the heart's confirmation—revelation can come in different ways—but *always* the impression will *feel* good and right and clear. On the other hand, if our thoughts are wrong, "you shall have no such feelings [of peace and joy in the heart], but you shall have a stupor of thought that shall cause you to forget the thing which is wrong" (D&C 9:8–9). In other words, the mind and heart will not be in harmony. While we may not actually forget totally the mistaken idea, we may be unclear or uneasy about it. It will feel like a "square peg in a round hole," troubling and discomforting us.

These are basic guides as to what each person must learn to know and feel for himself or herself. They will always be present in revelation, even in the spectacular kind, for "this is the spirit of revelation; behold, this is the spirit by which Moses brought the children of Israel through the Red Sea on dry ground" (D&C 8:3). Apparently even such a remarkable manifestation of God's power came to Moses first in his mind and in his heart.

There are many people who want revelation to be more sensational than this simple, unobservable process. Some do seem to be more prone to visions, dreams, and heavenly voices in their communications with the other side, but most of us just plug along listening to that "still small voice" in our thoughts and feelings. Brigham Young espoused a practical philosophy, which he expressed to a visiting journalist: "The highest inspiration is good sense—the knowing what to do, and how to do it" (as quoted in Leonard J.

Arrington, *Brigham Young: American Moses* [New York: Alfred A. Knopf, 1985], p. 328). Thus we should never feel somehow inferior or unacceptable because we don't receive the more dramatic manifestations that some people relate.

Indeed, one should perhaps be leery of persons who continually speak of intimate spiritual experiences as if they were common daily fare. There are also some who tend to inflate subtle promptings into breathtaking "spiritual experiences." Not only is this discouraging to others who may think there is something wrong with them because they are not thus favored, but also such people may be setting themselves up as a light for others to follow, and they may lead right out of the Church those who are looking for the spectacular over the simple. Elder Boyd K. Packer has addressed this problem in his thoughtful address, "The Candle of the Lord." "I have learned that strong, impressive spiritual experiences do not come to us very frequently. And when they do, they are generally for our own edification, instruction, or correction. . . . I have come to believe also that it is not wise to continually talk of unusual spiritual experiences. They are to be guarded with care and shared only when the Spirit itself prompts us to use them to the blessing of others." (*That All May Be Edified* [Salt Lake City: Bookcraft, 1982], p. 337.)

What Is Spirituality?

An often-asked question in the Church is, What is spirituality? If relating great spiritual manifestations is not necessarily a sign of spirituality and living by the Spirit, what is? The answer is not always readily apparent. We often entertain mistaken ideas about what constitutes a "spiritual" life.

Twenty years ago Wendy went to Israel for a week as a BYU student. Like many others, she wanted to have great spiritual experiences at the important holy sites. She wanted the one at the Garden Tomb to be the most rewarding and climactic of all. She stood with a few friends before what may have been Golgotha, reading the crucifixion account from Elder James E. Talmage's *Jesus the Christ*. As she got to the really heart-wrenching part she became self-consciously concerned that she wasn't being moved to tears. As far as she understood, tears and spiritual experiences always went together. Lest her epiphany pass her by, she squeezed out a few tears just to assure herself and those with her that she was a spiritual person.

Seven years, one husband, three children, and a good dose of reality later, she was back at the Garden Tomb with a tour of seminary and institute teachers and their spouses. They were allowed to hold a testimony meeting in a private area there. She felt overwhelmed at the privilege of bearing testimony of Christ in that sacred place. This time the tears came freely—even uncontrollably. She was choking back the tears and it was all she could do to keep from sobbing out loud like a baby. She got the emotional response she had wanted, but from the two experiences she learned that tears are not always appropriate in a spiritual moment.

In June of 1993 she departed for her third experience in the Holy Land—living in Jerusalem for a year while Brent taught at the BYU Jerusalem Center. She was looking forward to sharing those great spiritual outpourings with our children. She quickly discovered that living there is not nearly so romantic as visiting while staying in four-star hotels. It was very hard physical and emotional work. When she visited the Garden Tomb this time all was peaceful, but she felt nothing special.

After being in Jerusalem a month or so she began to wonder if she was ever again going to feel those awe-inspiring "Holy Land" feelings that all the students and tour groups were raving about and that she too had once felt. In fact, after a whole year there she had rarely had a strong spiritual witness at any of the holy sites. One Sabbath, however, several weeks after arriving in Israel, when she was feeling spiritually barren, the student choir arose and sang: "I am a child of God and He has sent me here. . . . Lead me, guide me, walk beside me. Help me find the way." She was somewhat disconcerted because their eyes were filled with so much beauty and light and they seemed to be singing directly to her. The spiritual witness came unbidden. She then understood that her own spiritual growth would no longer come from visiting holy places but rather from leading and helping others to have the life-changing experiences in Israel and in life that she had already enjoyed.

We offer these three experiences in the Holy Land as a sort of metaphor for measuring one's growth in learning about spirituality—from the outward show to the inward reality. Here we also share some other principles we have gleaned from the scriptures, the prophets, and our own faltering attempts to become spiritual beings.

Sometimes it takes a lot of maturing to realize that tears may or may not accompany an outpouring of the Spirit. In fact, we have come to prefer the deep, quiet inner peace which is not visible to others but which may represent an even more profound and life-altering experience. Further, we have learned that the tearful response evinced by sensational or sentimental stories and songs may be emotional rather than spiritual and does not have the literal power to build spirituality that scripture, sacred hymns, and other divinely inspired writings do. Joseph F. McConkie, Professor of Ancient Scripture at Brigham Young University, warned that there are some in the Church who "ride on an emotional wave. If it brings a tear to your eye or raises the hair on your arms, it must be revelation. They love the sensational and the dramatic but quickly lose interest in the scriptures and the basic principles of the gospel. They cherish 'hand-me-down' stories that they hold to tenaciously even when confronted by eyewitnesses who tell them their stories are embellished and inaccurate." (*The Spirit of Revelation* [Salt Lake City: Deseret Book Co., 1985], p. 127.)

We likewise have discovered that many of the undocumented but spiritually titillating stories which circulate and recirculate through the Church are Mormon folklore at best, and outright fabrications at worst, even though they have been written up and copied off. One needs to be on guard against these spiritual counterfeits that create a foundation of sand rather than of rock (see Matthew 7:24–27).

Neither do we have to speak in hushed tones or use pious phrases in order to demonstrate spirituality. It is important to know when to speak with genuine reverence, but the Spirit is what carries our message to the hearts of our listeners, not a manipulation of the tone of voice or the mannerisms of speech.

Long-faced solemnity and an over-serious manner are not required to make us truly spiritual individuals, either. Elder George A. Smith warned: "When a man professes a great deal of sanctity—a great deal of holiness and piety,—when he can scarcely speak without a pious groan, he is to be suspected; for such hypocrisy is in itself the most cursed corruption that can exist" (*Journal of Discourses* 7:116). The Spirit never makes us uptight or stilted; rather it fills us with joy and good humor. Even spiritual moments can be deeply enhanced by joyous laughter when the timing is right. Indeed, the prophets and General Authorities of the Church seem to enjoy the most delightful sense of humor.

We have already made the point that a strict outward observance of the commandments does not necessarily mean inward spirituality, either, as demonstrated in the lives of the scribes and the Pharisees of Jesus' day. Again, it takes spiritual maturity to move from living the letter of the law, which is usually more noticeable to others, to living by the Spirit, which is always more pleasing to the Lord. Frederic W. Farrar, author of the well-respected work *The Life of Christ,* observed:

> It is easy to be a slave to the letter, and difficult to enter into the spirit; easy to obey a number of outward rules, difficult to enter intelligently and self-sacrificingly into the will of God; easy to entangle the soul in a network of petty observances, difficult to yield the obedience of an enlightened heart; easy to be haughtily exclusive, difficult to be humbly spiritual; easy to be an ascetic or a formalist, difficult to be pure, and loving, and wise, and free; easy to be a Pharisee, difficult to be a disciple; very easy to embrace a self-satisfying and sanctimonious system of rabbinical observances, very difficult to love God with all the heart, and all the might, and all the soul, and all the strength. (*The Life of Christ* [Salt Lake City: Bookcraft, 1994], p. 445.)

Finally, we have discovered that many of the spiritual experiences we traditionally have used to measure spirituality—revelations, visions, healings, and so forth—are actually lesser manifestations of the Spirit in our lives. In teaching about the gifts of the Spirit, the Prophet Joseph taught that the most visible gifts are the ones that are "most sought after," but that "the greatest, the best, and the most useful gifts would be known nothing about by an observer" (*History of the Church* 5:30). While we can be saved without ever having had any of these more outward demonstrations of spiritual gifts, we can never be saved without the imperative inward gifts—the testimony of Jesus Christ, a broken heart and a contrite spirit, repentance and forgiveness, being born again, faith, hope, and above all, charity.

Charity— The Ultimate Measure of Spirituality

In our search for spirituality, we (Wendy and Brent) feel that the Lord has been teaching us that charity—the pure love of Christ, love like Christ's—is the hallmark and ultimate measure of spirituality. The scriptures make it unmistakably clear that, as Paul teaches Timothy, "the end of the commandment is charity out of a pure heart" (1 Timothy 1:5). Christ taught that loving God and neighbor as oneself are the most important things we can learn to do, and all other laws and words of the prophets hang on and point to these two commandments of charity (see Matthew 22:36–40).

Both Paul and Mormon attest that charity is even greater than faith and hope and all other spiritual gifts we can attain in this life. Paul declared: "Though I speak with the tongues of men and of angels, and have not charity, I am become as sounding brass, or a tinkling cymbal. And though I have the gift of prophecy, and understand all mysteries, and all knowledge; and though I have all faith, so that I could remove mountains, and have not charity, I am nothing." (1 Corinthians 13:1–2.) Though we may outwardly appear and/or sound very spiritual, if we have not charity inwardly we have missed the whole point of the gospel of Jesus Christ—the gospel of love. Pure love is the most Christlike spiritual quality we can develop, and when we love as he would love we are closest to doing his will.

However, developing charity and thus true spirituality is as difficult as it is important. Like the oil of righteousness in the lamps of the five wise virgins, it comes only drop by drop. There are no short cuts, no great spiritual manifestations that suddenly transform us into spiritual giants. Charity, which as noted in previous chapters comes to us as a gift, comes gradually, even painstakingly, as we pay the price in daily efforts and after we have prayed continually for it with all the energy of our hearts, as Mormon teaches us we must (see Moroni 7:48). It is not just a lofty philosophy, but must come to permeate all our desires, thoughts, and actions.

Our favorite example of this kind of love in everyday actions is told by George Durrant in his own words.

> Shortly after arriving in . . . [Korea after the Korean War], I observed that some people were excited about Christ and his teachings, but at the same time, the Koreans were confused because the good they had read and heard about Christianity was quite different

from the questionable conduct observed in soldiers who supposedly were Christians.

Korean civilians came into our camp each day to perform the menial tasks that were undesirable to us, such as K. P. They, in turn, were paid, and the arrangements made both groups happy. As they went about our camp they, like us, used the dirt paths that led between the weeds and other growth. When American soldiers and Koreans met on the paths, the Koreans jumped aside into the weeds while the soldiers proudly passed by.

As I observed this situation, it occurred to me that this was not the way things should be. This was their land, and we, if anyone, should move off the paths. Therefore, I made it a practice to move aside and let the Koreans pass on the path. They seemed amazed but also pleased. Soon I learned many of their names, and as they passed I greeted them by name.

Months passed and I learned some of the ways that the GI's had created to communicate with the Koreans. One rather unusual system consisted of a way to describe the goodness or badness of something by calling that which was very good "number one" and that which was very bad "number ten." . . .

It was a rule at our camp that if a soldier held the rank of corporal or higher, he would enter the mess hall and go to a table where a Korean worker would bring him his meal. All who had lesser rank went through the line for their own food.

One day I entered the hall, noticed the line was long, and sat down at a table with five of my friends who were eating while I waited for the line to get shorter. As I talked to the others at the table, I felt someone at my elbow. I looked up, and standing at my side with a tray of food was one of the Korean workers. I realized that he was about to put the tray before me, so I pointed to the stripe on my arm and said, "You can't serve me. I'm just a private."

He looked down at me with moistened eyes and quietly said, "I serve you. You a 'number one' Christian!" (*Inspirational Missionary Stories*, Leon R. Hartshorn, comp. [Salt Lake City: Deseret Book Co., 1976], pp. 15–16.)

However, charity, like spirituality, is not always completely measurable in outward actions. Paul warns us that though we bestow all of our goods to feed the poor and even sacrifice our lives, and yet have not charity, we are nothing (see 1 Corinthians 13:3). On the other hand, at times when we cannot serve physically we will still be blessed if, spiritually, we possess the pure love of Christ.

Thus charity and spirituality are not something one has to make an effort to display. In fact, it is probable that the more we try to make a show of them, the less we have. Spirituality is something we are at the very core. It may be measured in how closely we resemble Jesus Christ. Mormon tells us that to be like him when he appears, we must be filled with charity (see Moroni 7:48).

Accordingly, we (Wendy and Brent) learned that the message of the Holy Land is not about having spiritual experiences in holy places at all, but about loving and serving people. Everything that the pre-mortal Jehovah and the mortal Messiah, Jesus Christ, did in that land he did because of his perfect love for people. Likewise, genuine spirituality is not measured by whether we have spiritual manifestations at the right time or in the right places, but by how we love people. Like Peter the impetuous Apostle, Wendy learned that the meaning of her spiritual seasoning and of all spiritual gifts and manifestations can be summed up in the Savior's simple directive, "Feed my sheep" (see John 21:15–17).

Thus all roads of righteousness eventually lead us to this pure, Christlike love. It is the culminating result of all our faithful thoughts and actions. It is also the answer to our problems and the most effective tool in changing our lives and the lives of those around us.

Further, while living by the Spirit is the grand key to the inward stillness and healing we are seeking in our lives and in writing this book, charity is the sweetest of all the fruits of that Spirit, the crowning virtue of a spiritual life, and the vessel of our ultimate perfection and peace. In the Doctrine and Covenants the Lord concludes a lengthy list of counsel and commandments for his new Saints with this simple, reassuring admonition: "Above all things, clothe yourselves with the bond of charity, as with a mantle, which is the bond of perfectness and peace." (D&C 88:125).

Charity never faileth, endless fount of love,
Springing pure and perfect from pristine realms
    above;
Love that asks no merit, no promise or requite,
Love that kindles faith and hope, virtue, strength,
    and light.

Charity granteth power, charity bringeth peace,
Love that casteth out all fear and sweetly breathes
    release;
Frees from chains of hatred, confusion, vengeance,
    strife.
Charity—the mantle soft that cloaks the pain of life.

Charity reigns supernal, exceeding faith and hope.
Pure love endows the humblest life with height and
    depth and scope.

For though I speak with angels and pious heights
    attain,
If these stem not from charity, then empty is my gain.

Charity seeks the stranger with coarse or foreign
    ways,
The neighbors, friends, and loved ones who may try
    my patient days;
The enemy and derelict, for more like Christ I'll be
When compassion swells my bosom unconditionally.

Charity, priceless gift of God for followers of Christ,
Aim of ceaseless, reaching prayer and selfhood
    sacrificed;
If I am in his image when he appears above
'Twill be the face of charity, for God, himself, is love.

                    —Wendy C. Top

Index